FINERMAN'S RULES

Secrets I'd Only Tell My Daughters About Business and Life

KAREN FINERMAN

GRAND CENTRAL
PUBLISHING

NEW YORK   BOSTON

Business Plus
Hachette Book Group
237 Park Avenue
New York, NY 10017

www.HachetteBookGroup.com

Printed in the United States of America

RRD-C

First Edition: June 2013
10 9 8 7 6 5 4 3 2 1

Business Plus is an imprint of Grand Central Publishing.
The Business Plus name and logo are trademarks of Hachette Book Group, Inc.

The publisher is not responsible for websites (or their content) that are not owned by the publisher.

Library of Congress Control Number: 2013932310

To my late mother, Jane:
You taught me everything I needed to know,
except how to stop missing you.

To Lucy, Jack, William, and Kate:
I couldn't love you more, and yet every day, I do.

To Lawrence:
All these years later you're still the "one"—
always were, always will be. None of it works
without you.

CONTENTS

CHAPTER 1

What Are Successful Girls Really Made Of?

I was raised a Calvinist. You might think you know what that means, but let me explain it the way my mother preached it to my three sisters and me back when we were at home: "I buy my girls Calvin Klein clothes, so that's all they know. Then when they graduate from college, they have to figure out how to pay for them themselves."

That's it—that's the philosophy. I can't tell you how many people I meet who think Calvinism is something else entirely. It worked for us.

Wendy, the oldest, went on to be a movie producer of such films as *The Devil Wears Prada*, *Stepmom*, and *Forrest Gump*, for which she won an Oscar. Unlike many people in the movie business, Wendy knew no one to help her get started. Through sheer will, she managed to find a job working for Steve Tisch, the producer. And it was only through her relentless perseverance and ambition that she finally got the book *Forrest Gump* made into one of the most successful films of all time.

My brother Mark, the second oldest, was spared the Calvinist lecture. Yet he still managed to become a real estate financier of such success and renown that I can scarcely come across someone in the real estate business who doesn't know him and tell me with a smile, "I love your brother." After a brief career as a professional tennis player on the pro circuit, Mark realized he could teach others how to play tennis to make money, or he could learn business skills and teach himself how to make money.

He went from teaching a real estate king how to hit topspin to realizing he could be the real estate mogul himself, and he already knew how to play tennis. He became the right-hand man to two big real estate players, first at Nomura and then Credit Suisse, before becoming the number-one man himself in the CMBS business (commercial mortgage-backed securities—don't worry if you don't know what that is), financing office towers and shopping malls— and he went higher from there. Yet he is still, at heart, the boy I grew up with. Even though he lives in a grown-up house in grown-up Greenwich, Connecticut, he's like Tom Hanks in *Big*. Mark has every toy imaginable—cars, horses, pinball machines, tree houses, go-carts, vegetable gardens, an indoor basketball court, candy machines—and he still thinks cartoons are funny.

Then there's me, the tomboy, nerd, and hedge fund co-founder.

And pulling up the rear—our two little sisters. First is Leslie, who followed my footsteps into finance after graduating from Berkeley and headed to Morgan Stanley. She then made the leap to become an analyst at a large credit hedge fund. Leslie recently took the road less traveled (in our family) and became a stay-at-home mom (for now). Leslie is the arbiter of cool in our family, the master of style. She can renovate an apartment and act as a general contractor even when nine months pregnant.

Last is Stacey, the youngest, maybe the smartest of us all, who was hired out of Wharton by Salomon Brothers, then got plucked away by RBS, and then after the 2008 market crash was hired by Goldman Sachs. After a breakup with a boyfriend, she decided to channel the energy left over after her day job to become a world-class Ironman competitor. She transformed herself into an extraordinary endurance machine. She doesn't just focus on finishing in the allotted 17 hours. She's looking to improve on her personal best of 12 hours, for the 2.4 mile swim, the 112 mile bike ride, and the 26.2 mile marathon.

Funnily, we all made our way from laid-back Southern California to New York City and its environs. It was here that we hoped we would find our success.

Instilling in her children her own brand of Calvinism, our mom didn't subscribe to the Happiness-Is-a-Warm-Puppy, Free-to-Be-You-and-Me parenting styles that were so prevalent when we were growing up. I think she may have truly believed that being only warm and loving to your children conveyed that you accepted them as they were, as opposed to putting forth the effort to make them better. She always let us know that we could—and should—reach for more, with our academics, sports interests, and our ambitions. If you had asked my mother, "Would you rather your children be successful or happy?" she would have answered, without the slightest bit of hesitation, "Successful. How can you be happy if you're not?"

Growing up, that message stuck with me. It was so imbedded in my thoughts that I don't ever remember when I learned it. It just was. Any of my friends who spent time in our kitchen (the neighborhood meeting place) heard the same message. In the way other mothers would have said, "Did you get enough to eat?" or "Any crushes these days?" my mother would say to some of my seemingly less ambitious friends, "How are you going to support yourself with no plan?"

As a teenager, rather than setting myself on a course to pursue fame (quite common growing up in L.A., the entertainment capital of the world), happiness, fulfillment, and spiritual enlightenment (also quite common), I skipped right on to trying to be successful. Let's just get on with it, I felt. "Onward" became my motto.

I wanted to get out in the world, have a great job, make my mark, and see how far I could go. And I wanted to make good on the philosophy my mother drilled into us with all the subtlety of a Lady Gaga performance. I got it loud and clear. I would need to succeed, and then I could possibly be happy.

* * *

And so I set about a career with a goal to make money, be independent, and make a success of myself on Wall Street. But as I did that, I realized that what I learned on Wall Street could be used anywhere, and in any part of my life. It's OK to have a plan, to invest in your future—for your financial security, your love life, your personal fulfillment, and even your happiness. To have personal happiness as a stated goal doesn't detract from it if you get there. Serendipity is nice, but hoping for luck and the magic of happenstance shouldn't be an excuse for a lack of proactivity. I had to learn for myself that waiting isn't a life plan.

In my journey to succeed and find happiness, I've accumulated a fair amount of wisdom as I saw what made some people quite successful, while others, who were far more talented, got stuck, paralyzed, or repeated the same mistakes over and over. I saw, too often, how women consistently got in their own way. That's what this book is about. It's my story and the lessons I've learned—with some wisdom from friends, siblings, and colleagues mixed in—about how I knew what I wanted but needed to learn to get out of my own way. Since the steps to success (in business and life) didn't come naturally to me (and really, look at the messes around you; do they for anyone?), I had to try, then fail and try again. I had to come up with principles and "rules" to add to the Calvinist ethic I got from my mother. And it's not easy, because people don't tell you what to expect—especially women, who believe they are not supposed to say out loud some of the things that other women *really* need to hear. I don't care if what I have to say is PC or not. As I started writing this book, I realized my children didn't know and hadn't even considered what I thought I had already so thoroughly engrained in them, which is that they will need to be independent and self-reliant. They will need to be in charge of their lives. These are things they need to know.

What I wanted was very clear to me—success. To me—and I hope for you—that *does* mean money. I want you to have enough money and the independence that money affords so it isn't a force determining what you can and can't do, or who you can and can't be. Plus, having money is fun. I remember the absolute, joyous freedom I felt when I first went to college: I had no bedtime, no curfew, no rules—I loved it. I was in charge. I couldn't believe I didn't have to answer to anyone.

Then four and a half years later, I would feel the same excitement when I made my first bonus. All the money was mine to spend (or save) as I wished. It was that same absolute joy of not having to answer to anyone. That $6,000 bonus was my first feeling of being successful as a grown-up. As I climbed the ladder in finance, the amounts grew, but that thrill of success at that very first bonus has always been the most memorable and meaningful.

* * *

I have spent much of my life where the boys are, first as a tomboy and then on Wall Street. Growing up, I loved every and any sport. I was frustrated by girls who didn't, so I spent most of my afternoons with the boys. In middle school, I was allowed to enroll in the boys PE—65 hardly developed boys and me. It never occurred to me that they could do anything I couldn't. And that's the way it was until high school when I joined the girls' tennis team.

In spite of my affinity for sports, as a teenager it started to dawn on me that I wasn't really going to become a professional athlete. The claustrophobic milieu and some of the overbearing parents definitely weren't for me, and somehow I was sensing that I might not be *that* good—that is, good enough to go all the way.

But with my mother and upbringing, I knew I needed a plan. Subliminally, I was looking for what I would be when I grew up, but I didn't have a guide.

I saw my mother as determined and passionate as a parent and teacher, but she was also a seemingly powerless mom. I had seen how the person who makes the money has the power, whether or not they wielded it with a heavy hand. My dad did well financially—as a well-known and highly respected orthopedic surgeon (and team doctor for UCLA football and basketball)—but he still struggled under the weight of all those children. The net result was that I learned that money isn't infinite—it's limited and limiting—and that I never wanted to be in a position where I had to ask a man (or anyone) for money. I wanted a freedom my mother didn't have. Money was the way to get that, as well as just a good thing to have. I remember my mother (who liked to imagine herself as a talented interior designer) coming home with a love seat she thought was perfect and my father telling her it was too expensive. I could see that she was crushed and embarrassed to have to take it back. I hated seeing her demoralized. If only she didn't need to ask him for the money.

With that desire of financial independence firmly in mind when I was 15, something caught my eye. It was a front-page article in the *Los Angeles Times* business section with a big glamorous photo highlighting Ivan Boesky, the famous Wall Street risk arbitrageur, long before he was convicted of insider trading. I was enthralled by the excitement and action of trading stocks of companies involved in takeover deals. He was a titan of Wall Street who sat at the center of high-stakes trading and gigantic amounts of money. And it was his for the taking, if he just made smart bets. It didn't even seem that hard; anyone could do it. In fact, I could do it.

Just like that, I knew. I wanted to be a risk arbitrageur. *Ar-be-tra-zher*—I loved the sound of it. I wanted to be in the action, and I wanted to be the one making lots of money. I loved the image of creating my own destiny and being in control of my world. This wasn't some fantasy future in the way lots of girls announce that they want to be a fashion designer or a singer. I had found my calling. This was going to happen. I was destined for Wall Street.

I informed my parents that I intended to apply only to the Wharton School at the University of Pennsylvania, as that was the surest route to Wall Street. If I didn't get in, I wasn't going to college.

This was one of the more memorable in a series of stupid risk/reward plans I would make in life. Fortunately, Wharton accepted me. I remember heading off to college with the implicit, though unspoken, message from my mother: "Don't come home till you've set the world on fire."

Fast-forward till now: a lot of things have worked out better than I could have hoped. I've worked hard *and* I've been exceedingly lucky, and I've failed more than a few times.

Here's what's worked: I have a family I love—two sets of boy-girl twins (Jack and Lucy, born in '97, and Kate and William, '01). I have a husband, Lawrence Golub, I didn't let get away, who for better or worse (and we've had both) is the love of my life. I have friends I've known since grade school, high school, college, and after who inspire me and make me laugh and accept me fully. And last, and not least, I have a career that has brought me much of what I've hoped for in terms of money, freedom, influence, and excitement, including my added role on the CNBC show *Fast Money*, where I get to weigh in about the market and investing.

Here's what hasn't worked: For years I thought I wasn't successful enough and worried about whether people thought I was, and it drained a lot of energy and created a lot of stress. I was pregnant with twins. Twice. For some reason, I managed to have two pregnancies that tested all of my physical, mental, and marital strength. (Who knew the fertility clinic would be the "fun" part.) I've fumbled in business more times than I care to admit, both in investing and in leading. I've dealt with the near death of our business—when we couldn't blame it on a global market crash but on our own mistakes and egos. I suffered from guilt (oddly, only mild) over being a working mom, though I'm fully over that now. And I never, never have downtime. Going forward, I know there's a future of obstacles, mistakes, and life's misfortunes ahead, but I can't worry about that now.

Here's the thing I wasn't expecting—that finding success investing and being on Wall Street could be in any way instructive to finding happiness and "success" in the rest of my life. I wasn't expecting portfolio management decisions to be metaphors for life decisions, yet that's exactly what I found. Working in a male-dominated industry only brought these insights into sharper focus. Your industry may be different than mine. Your life may be different than mine, but I want you to recognize where women are at a disadvantage and help you avoid those traps. I don't want to waste time bemoaning the disparities between men and women, or the challenges for women if you are in a male-dominated field. Learn what you can from men.

I want you to learn the value of taking away just one thing of worth from someone else's screwup or triumph. Maybe you won't need to learn from your own stupidity if you can learn from mine. And frankly, I'd be honored if you did. There are choices to be made along the road that improve the likelihood of success—both in work and in the delicate balance of work and everything else. You can actually make things easier on yourself, especially when you're honest with yourself and others. There are ways to make decisions that improve your chances of success. There is real-world knowledge about taking risks—risks that are always there, so why not consider how to handle them rather than avoid or succumb to decisions not of your choosing. And we can learn to deal head-on with our squeamishness about putting ourselves out there—which too often feels tainted or wrong rather than natural and right.

CHAPTER 2

Get Out of Your Own Way

The biggest obstacle women face in their careers is themselves. From our start in the working world, too many of us make decisions that don't take into account the possibility—let alone the probability—that we can succeed. Even the most well educated and hard-charging should just assume that as a woman you're going to have a harder time. There's going to be more on your plate than any guy in your office. It is just a fact, or as my friend Janet often says, "Soccer would be easier if you could use your hands. But you can't."

I remember trying to explain to my son Jack after he came back disheartened from a soccer loss that complaining about unfairness is a waste. He was upset about the ref, the mud, how his team got unfairly penalized, and on and on. I looked at him unswayed and repeated the truism: "And soccer would be easier if you could use your hands. But you can't." He looked back at me equally unswayed and said, "But mom, I'm the goalie." After a brief laugh at the irony of the lesson I was trying to make, the point remains: Life is hard; complaining rarely improves things.

There are barriers to success and it's difficult for everyone, but we need to get over the misleading beliefs and unnecessary obstacles we put in our own way.

I know we can't rationalize or wish away the differences between the sexes. Beyond our upbringing, conditioning, training, and institutional expectations, and/or our own internal aspirations for a division of labor with our partner, it's in our biological hardwiring. If an infant cries in the middle of the night, the father *may* wake up and wish he could do something about it, but a woman can't *not* hear the cry, and if she's breast-feeding, she lactates. Same stimulus, very different response.

My approach has always been to focus on reality and not belabor the inequality. The road to success is just different for women. There are enough hurdles for women already to being successful. We need to get out of our own way and create more options, not fewer. Through trial and error I've learned that success starts when you develop the nerve to ask for what you want and develop a sense of intuition for what your boss, colleagues, and clients need.

We do ourselves a great disservice by throwing self-made artificial roadblocks in our path, from our complex relationship to the concept of success, to our resistance to standing out and wanting to be noticed, to that especially challenging start to our careers where we may stall waiting for the "perfect" job or shortchange ourselves by equating our careers with dating and hoping we'll get "picked." Too often women fall prey to the idea that, "If it's right, it will happen," an idea that we apply to the right job, the right apartment, or the right partner. That is a big mistake.

We all need to give ourselves permission to succeed wildly and to stand out, and we need to stop pretending we don't have goals and dreams. We need to develop the nerve to ask for what we want. We have to do these things focused on ourselves, not in comparison to others—including men.

Untangling the Desire to Succeed

Let's start with the very big obstacle of feeling like it's unflattering to *want* to be successful and to want to win. (For lots of women, it's OK to *be* successful but the *wanting* is what gets in our way.) Yet it doesn't take a sociological study to know this:

If you don't proactively want success for yourself, how are you going to convince others that you're worthy of attaining it?

No matter what our aspirations—to be the first woman president, to invent a breakthrough medicine, to be in charge of the first mission that lands a human on Mars, or the more realistic and likely goals of leading departments, universities, and our own start-ups and investment funds—we can make the idea of success unattainable, too hard, and not even that desirable. But success—and the financial wealth that can come with it—opens doors. Success creates options, which are some of the most valuable things you can have. So let's begin:

Act as if, believe as if, plan as if you can and will succeed. There is no reason not to.

I remember confessing to my friend Peter—whom I had met in our Yuppie-filled Upper East Side apartment building in the 1980s—after one of our many Sunday-night spaghetti dinners (that he cooked) that I wanted to be the most successful woman on Wall Street. I've fallen far short of that but well ahead of where I'd have been if I had no aspirations, no big goals, and no plan. It might have been a bit grandiose, but it was true. We accept this desire in performers, teachers, and athletes. Many women unabashedly want to be the best mother they can be. And we all believe that wish is noble, right, and necessary. Why, then, is it shameful to want to be the best _____(fill in your profession)_____? Ask more of yourself and you shall receive.

The corollary of women not giving themselves permission to want to succeed—and even win—at whatever they set their sights on is that women are too good at losing. One of the most inexplicable phenomena to me is the notion that it is unappealing for women to want to win. There is no shame in winning and no shame in wanting to win.

The pinnacle of this ridiculousness is evidenced by the Miss America Pageant. At the very end, the last two contestants are on stage waiting together to hear who will be crowned the next Miss America (let's leave aside for now the inherent sexism in the pageant itself). When they announce the runner-up, she has to pretend to be so happy for the winner. It's absurd—you don't see that in the Super Bowl.

Why aren't we allowed to want to win? Is it seen as too aggressive? Too competitive and risky to our relationships with men? Or too risky to our own definitions of women? I'm not going to solve that issue; I just want to admit that I want to win. I want to outperform. You will likely feel the same way if you let yourself—at least in some parts of your life. It actually makes me nervous if I feel that I am caring a bit less about winning as I age.

Wanting to win shows a desire to work hard and a willingness to make sacrifices. If you're a manager of anything (a department, a baseball team, a small business), do you want to create the best team of gracious runners-up that you can?

And for just a second, let's be honest about "winning" and "success." Of course, "success" covers all those higher callings of influence, status, meaning, good works, and fulfilling relationships. But it also covers money—that is, making it. Too often, to soften the meaning of "success," we round off the meaning, as if it's impolite to want financial success, or at least to talk about it. But the financial rewards that come with success create more opportunities, freedom, and choices than almost anything else. So do the work that matters to you most and that you'll thrive in, but don't discount the role of money in the success you seek.

When we're young, our heads are filled with a lot of nonsense like, "Follow your bliss" or "Do what you love and the money will follow" (this works as well as "Eat what you love and you'll love the way you look"). Well, if you're 45 years old and working for Save the Pandas and still can't pay off your student loans or go on a decent vacation or buy a primary residence, happiness may be on your personal endangered species list. If you happen to be a marketing executive and can afford to write a check to the World Wildlife Foundation and one day go Panda-watching in China, you might be happier.

Ask yourself these questions:

- What do you want, even if you tell no one? Taking away any concerns about pride, or what's realistic, or what's appropriate, what is the biggest professional goal you can imagine for yourself? Don't minimize that goal because you think it's unattractive.
- Which women are role models you can emulate? Are there men you can emulate? Did their anatomy get them where they are? If not, don't necessarily rule them out as a role model. But your first choice should be a woman. If you don't have a person who comes to mind, look for women in your family, your college, or among your friends' mothers, your mother's friends, or the media for role models that exhibit the qualities of success and winning that you can relate to and desire.

Stand Out, Be Noticed

To succeed, it is your duty to put yourself out there. I've learned the hard way. At heart, I'm a wallflower. I believe in myself and my talent, but deep down I remain afraid to step up, or rather peel myself away from the wall. But I do it anyway.

From the time I was a 10-year-old tomboy and the neighborhood kids played basketball, I would stand by the side of the court and hope they would ask if I wanted to play or that my brother would tell them to invite me. My mother would always push me to go ask them if I could join the game. If they would just give me a chance, I knew they would be impressed. (I later went on to become the Pepsi Hotshot

Basketball Competition winner for Southern California—which I won at a Lakers halftime after many regional victories. It was my debut and only appearance at the "Fabulous Forum" in downtown L.A.)

Both as a teenager and newly minted young professional, I remember hating to call a store to ask their hours, to stop a stranger on the street for directions, or to ask a shoe salesman for help. To this day, sending a dish back at a restaurant is nearly impossible for me, even if it has no resemblance whatsoever to what I ordered.

A first, small turning point came for me in eighth grade when I ran for president of the student body. I was an eighth grader at long last, a big fish in the small pond (not that small actually, with close to 1,000 kids) that was Hawthorne Elementary School, grades K through eight. Oddly, I have never really had a fear of public speaking. I prepared (what I thought was) a clever speech, which I presented as if I were Muhammad Ali. I wore a boxing robe and gloves and delivered it entirely in rhyme. It seemed to go over well, and I won the election. As an aside, "Finerman" is an excellent surname for running in eighth-grade elections. My slogan was "Who's the finest in the West? Finerman, she's the best." And there was "Finerman—the finer woman to represent our eighth grade."

Only after winning the election did it occur to me that I had to *be* the class president. I had to run the student council meetings, assign tasks to people, and the worst part, speak up to the powers that be at our school on behalf of our grade. Rather than be an advocate for our class, I would have far preferred to just say nothing and not put anyone out. But we wanted to be able to have school dances, hold a weekend car wash to raise money for a school trip, and expand the offering of doughnuts at our short morning break inappropriately named "Nutrition." Ironically, the students couldn't have chosen a person innately less inclined to ask for anything than me, but I had the job and I did it.

Years later, I still don't know if this reluctance to stand out is a woman thing or a shy-person thing, but it is particularly damaging to women. We need to push, slide, or adjust and find a way to stand out. I'm not advocating that anyone cross over into uber-bitch-in-stiletto-heels territory. But keep in mind that for every woman with a reputation for brashness or craftiness, there are dozens, hundreds of women still trying to muster the courage to stand out and be noticed.

The Finer Points

10 Highly Selective Guidelines for Public Speaking

1. Be prepared—*there is no substitute*. I practice every speech 10 times at least, even if it's a toast to a friend.

2. Be brief. Enough said.

3. Look at the venue beforehand.

4. Will you be wearing a mike? Know how it will hook on or if you will hold it.

5. Have an outfit you like.

6. Don't drink milk or milk products before you speak—they cause phlegm.

7. Expect to be nervous—don't think you're not going to be,

even having adhered to 1–6.

8. Keep a few good answers in your pocket for Q&A.

9. If you're small, make sure there's something to stand on.

10. Have your speech typed at least double-spaced and be sure pages are numbered.

Over the years, I've relapsed to wallflower many, many times. In every facet of my life, I felt more comfortable waiting by the side until someone noticed me, or asked me to dance, or to be on their science project team, or later to hire me, or hopefully even marry me. For me, every time I make a decidedly proactive move, it goes against my genetic code. I've just forced myself to do it so often that discipline has counteracted the gravitational pull toward the wall and triumphed over DNA. Imagine how you'll feel if you don't act. Don't expect to feel a surge of confidence—that never happens. Go to the downside—what's the worst that could happen?

It was a very long road for me to go from hanging back against the wall to publicly putting myself out there, but eventually I found my own way, and so can you.

My friend Joanna Coles, now the editor in chief of *Cosmopolitan*, is a master at standing out. She tells a wonderful story that will let you know that it's almost impossible to go too far. When she was a rising star in the glamorous world of women's magazines, she took a chance on boldness with a life-changing payoff:

I had been away on vacation and had not bothered to

check my voice messages. When I got home there was one from Cathie Black, who at the time was head of Hearst magazines, and she was asking to see me. She had suggested a time, only I picked up the message the day of the interview. I called that morning trying to reach her secretary, but no one picked up. I left a message saying I could be there and I tore off to buy a new outfit and have my hair blown out. When I arrived at the appointed hour I was told that, as they hadn't heard from me until that day, there had been a change of plan and Cathie was leaving for France and could no longer see me. In fact, she was leaving her apartment in a few minutes for the airport. I saw that as my opening. I asked if I could ride with her in the car to the airport. Her office called her and she said it was okay only if I could get to her apartment within the next five minutes. I roared out of the building, leapt into the middle of Sixth Avenue, stopped a cab and practically pried a poor passenger out. I arrived at her apartment just as her black Town Car was pulling away. My cab rode parallel until she saw me gesturing and had her car pull over to let me in. By the time we got to the airport I had the job at Marie Claire.

In my own quieter way, when I overcame my resistance to standing out, when I did it anyway, when I pushed myself, I was able to move to New York, to find the right guy, to cofound a hedge fund in 1992 (when there were no women doing that), to overcome infertility and fortunately give birth to two sets of twins, and to find a place for myself on TV.

My First Job

I had a summer job early in college working at Creative Artists Agency—Hollywood's most powerful talent agency. CAA, as it's known, was at the height of its omnipotence under its enigmatic then-CEO, Michael Ovitz. I was vaguely considering following my sister Wendy into the movie business. She and her now ex-husband, Mark Canton, who was a rising superstar at Warner Brothers Studios, got me the job. They were an ascending power couple in the business.

Though the allure of Wall Street was calling me, I was enamored by the glamour of Wendy's life and impressed by her meteoric rise as a producer in Hollywood. This was even before her enormous success winning an Oscar for *Forrest Gump*. Back then, she was the young, fresh-faced, witty, Wharton-educated ad exec who came to Hollywood and took the world by storm. Perhaps I already sensed her shoes were too big to fill (though, given the enormity of my feet, nobody's shoes are literally too big for me to fill).

It was my first real job anywhere, and I really didn't know what to expect. Prior to CAA, I had spent my summers competing in tennis tournaments or taking classes at Andover (a New England boarding school). I was excited to be getting paid the very round number of $5 an hour. In addition, I was eager to test myself in a corporate, albeit entertainment-style, setting, what with my one year at Wharton taking the basics of Economics under my belt. Business, in the textbook sense, felt intuitive to me. It's empowering to think you know everything (as only a

19-year-old can), though I still was too shy to begin to set the world on fire.

I started the first day with what I instantly recognized as a crew of beautiful, entitled children of the rich and powerful. Just by chance, we were all young women—no men.

It was clear from the beginning that my fellow interns weren't looking to have serious jobs—ever. Decades before the Kardashians, they were the "in" crowd, always popping up at the right parties, the right concerts, the right restaurants, as if those activities were their jobs. I, on the other hand, didn't even realize for several weeks that there *was* an "in" crowd, let alone attain a silent invitation for membership. They were beautiful and popular and moneyed. I, however, was nerdy, on the periphery of popular, and not moneyed. Though my parents generously graced me with spending money, I did not have "play" money and definitely couldn't afford the air of money those girls breezily lived in. In the Alice in Wonderland world of Beverly Hills where I grew up as the daughter of a successful orthopedic surgeon, I felt assuredly middle class.

Right away, I could see that my peers' carefree summer nonchalance was in stark contrast to my seriousness in starting my first job, which only added to my dorkiness. We had lunch together the first few days, but being placed on different ends of the 22nd floor after the first week was enough to break the binds of those tenuous connections. I was going to be on my own, which was fine with me.

My very first assignment was a very unglamorous, quiet, behind-the-scenes job cataloguing scripts. I efficiently set about doing the rather mindless task and quickly finished the backlog within days. With no more work for me to do, the librarian said she didn't need me. I took no real initiative and waited for someone to come tell me what to do. I didn't even know who that would be. At one point, I just decided to sit in the reception area reading the paper. How could I be so shy on the one hand and so brazenly stupid on the other?

A young agent came out several hours later to tell me that it wasn't really a good idea to be there. I still cringe at the monumental poor judgment on my part of those few hours sitting front and center in the lobby of the all-powerful CAA. I thought I wasn't being seen, but I was. I stood out for all the wrong reasons.

Luckily, perhaps since none of the "it" girls were available, shortly thereafter I got "placed on a desk" of a newly promoted young agent (Richard Lovett, who now runs CAA). Up until that point, he was such a neophyte agent that he had no assistant, which meant I became his first one.

Being placed on a desk is actually a really good assignment for an intern. You need a brain. You need a good memory. And mostly, you need to pay attention so you don't screw up. There were other jobs available for those with other better-developed body parts, but this fit me best. I looked forward to the responsibility. I knew it was a great opportunity to see how the business really worked and felt like I could be helpful, and maybe shine. I realized I needed to dress better also. Wear what you want to be. In fact, the lessons from that job have lasted my whole career.

From what I'd already seen, I got the feeling that what agents mostly do is talk on the phone. There is a subtle unmistakable art to the phone-call ritual in Hollywood. Who calls whom and when, what time of day, and what that tells you about where you are in the hierarchy. And for some reason, people in Hollywood are too busy to dial their own phone. (This was eons before speed dial and iPhones.) The assistant dials, asks for whomever the agent wishes to speak to, and when/if that person picks up, says, "Hold on for Mr./Ms. Agent-that-I'm-Dialing-For." It was a level of pretense that I never got comfortable with. I discovered it was much more fun and the days more rewarding when I was out there being seen, peripherally involved in the action, though mostly as voyeur, than when I was tucked away in the library.

I remember one call between an agent and a client. Actually, I only heard the agent using a stern, parental tone as if speaking to an adolescent:

Agent: Listen, _____ [big TV star known for drunken, rowdy behavior], when you arrived on location last week they gave you a jeep. Where is that jeep now?

After getting noticed on the young agent's desk, I developed a reputation as a bright, ambitious Wharton student (quite a novelty, as there weren't any Wharton kids there—ever—amidst the sea of students from USC, UCLA, and some junior colleges of ill repute). The one thing I did well that got me noticed was I thought about what the agent would need me to do next. I asked myself the question, What would he want next after the last call he just made? What next step did that last call trigger? Often I would ask him if he would like me to do what I had imagined his next request would be. The strategy worked. He was impressed that I was anticipating the next move. Sometimes it's not so hard to impress.

I saw that to be a good agent, you needed to be part psychotherapist, part friend, part school principal, and part partner in crime. I learned the etiquette of lying to your client, the Tom Sawyer technique of trying to sell your project to someone who only wants it because they think someone else (who isn't really prepared to close) does, and the art of ego management. Not once did I see an agent say to their client that this was not the client's best work. Typical would be this:

Agent: Hey Dudley [as in Moore], I just want to tell you how great *Best Defense* was. I saw it last night.

In reality, I would be shocked if any of you reading this have ever heard of or seen *Best Defense*. It was garbage.

To this day, what I value most is the criticism I get, for it is truthful—not the praise whose origin is unclear. The feedback I get from the producers about how I could have done a better job on a segment by being more forceful is valuable advice to me. "You look great" is of far less value.

I learned a lot and actually had fun and met lots of famous people. But I still remember so vividly wanting to hide, to not be seen. My natural inclinations kept pulling me down what would have been the wrong path.

I remember being invited to the *Ghostbusters* premiere. It was the biggest event of my tenure that summer. There were so many people that they screened the movie simultaneously in two side-by-side theaters in Westwood on Wilshire Boulevard. One theater was reserved for all the stars and VIPs, and one for everyone else. I went into the "everyone else" theater. Before the movie started, one of the young agents came in and tapped me on the shoulder and asked me if I wanted to go into the VIP theater. I awkwardly said, "No thanks," because I didn't feel comfortable. So dumb! I realized it a few minutes later but just sat silently through the movie.

I was so angry at myself that a few days later, when another of the young hotshot agents asked if I wanted to come out to a small casual party at a producer's house on Malibu beach, I pushed myself past my fear of feeling awkward and decided to go anyway. I had fun, but more importantly, after that weekend, young agents would invite me to go places, thinking, *Hey, let's invite the kid along*. Trust me. I wasn't one of the young hotties—that's not why they were inviting me. Maybe they wanted to ingratiate themselves to my sister and brother-in-law. Maybe they were just being nice. Or maybe there was another reason. It never occurred to me that they might have seen something in me that made them want to help me or possibly made them think that I could be a power player one day, and that could be good for them. It never crossed my mind that they might one day say, "I knew her when..."

Maybe I was afraid to stand out for fear of making a mistake, or what if someone thought I couldn't cut it, or what if I didn't fit in? What an idiot, filled with what ifs! I should have been asking, What if no one notices me? What if no one remembers my name or realizes I am here?

The most important thing I learned from that summer is this: Force yourself to stand out. You can't wait for it to feel natural and comfortable because that may never happen, and you can't learn to feel comfortable if you don't start trying. Whatever your next career (or life) goal is, you can leave everyone with the feeling that you're destined for big things and that they wish you'd stay. Don't let your desire to stay in your comfort zone or a rigid idea of your personality type get in the way of creating possibilities. I needed to learn this 100 times.

Even after I learned the lessons at CAA about standing out, and other times over and over, my natural reticence to do so still followed me to New York and into my first jobs. My misguided justification for not trying to stand out was that it was unbecoming and inappropriate for three reasons:

1. It's unflattering from the employer's point of view. (False. As an employer, I appreciate someone seeking to do more.)

2. It's not fair to the other employees. (Why are you worrying about them? They are not worrying about you.)

3. It just doesn't feel right to me. I don't like to toot my own horn. (Too bad—learn to do things that don't come naturally.)

Why do we need to be martyrs? I don't wish that for my daughters, and my mother didn't wish it for me, though she perfected Jewish martyrdom herself, always "sacrificing" for all her children and students at a school for bilingual inner-city kids where she taught first-grade reading. She always encouraged me to speak up. And she kept pushing me (as pushy Jewish mothers do), all the way into solid adulthood, prodding me to be more vocal, opinionated, and just to take my share of the airtime on the show. I was never the squeaky wheel growing up and certainly never in my family or in my early job, or even years into establishing our hedge fund. In fact, I took pride in my quiet. As an employer and a mother, I know the squeaky wheel gets the grease. As much as I hate to say it, it is undoubtedly true.

Consider ways you can stand out and be noticed:

- **Step away from the wall—metaphorically and actually.** You won't fall over. I swear. Speak up, volunteer, ask questions.
- **Discover where you can make your mark—and go there.** You DO have specific skills, talents, points of view, experiences to bring to everything you do. Some of these will make you more effective and more excited on the job.
- **Play ball.** Double entendre intended. This could literally mean joining the softball team or being a team player, pitching in. Volunteer for new assignments. Ask to be chosen. Stay late and put in the extra work.
- **Learn everything you can about the company and industry you work for.** This may allow you to add just one comment at a meeting or in a conversation that's eye-opening to someone else. And it can't hurt to get a universal context for your job.
- **Anticipate your boss's needs.** Pay attention to what your boss is working on, who is calling and emailing, what is coming up on the calendar. You'll be surprised at how much you can do to help if you make it your job to know what is going on.
- **Dress as if you are being seen—not as if you're invisible.**

You are always being noticed, even if it's as the girl who hides in the corner or the woman who shows too much cleavage, which leads me to a few thoughts on how to use your sexuality—wisely.

Use Your Sexuality

Being a woman at times bestows upon us a useful advantage. We'd be stupid not to use it. I'm not suggesting running out to try to sleep with every higher-up you can, though that has been effective for some—for me, after four kids, I'm not that interested in widening the circle of people who see me naked, nor is anyone begging me to abandon my clothes. I am saying don't try to hide your sexuality. You *cannot* be a woman out in the working world and not think about this. Do you remember the character Andy, the heroine in *The Devil Wears Prada* (a Wendy Finerman production, of which I am enormously proud)? She tries hard to *not* look fashionable. That was her statement. She wanted to be a true journalist, and her unspoken motto was, "I am trying so hard to not care how I look because I hate the notion of something so superficial mattering to me." Are you ever guilty of doing the same thing when it comes to your sexuality? I was. I never wore makeup, never even owned lipstick. I remember going to buy lipstick just before I was married. I was at the counter at Bergdorf Goodman and I asked for lipstick—revealing my naiveté, I failed to mention a brand or color. And the woman snidely questioned, "Are you from New York?"

Like my mother used to say, and I now subscribe to the sentiment wholeheartedly, "Would it kill you to wear a nice dress every once in a while?" Spend the effort and time and money—it's worth it. Plus, there's one added benefit: A friend from college used to wear a coat and tie to final exams. When I asked him why, he said, "Look sharp, be sharp." I got it. When you look good, you feel better, more confident, taller, sharper, sexier, and you act that way.

Men use their "tools" for bonding, whether it's sports, drinks, and maybe even attending the occasional strip club, so use yours. For me, though, I am not one of those women who ever felt comfortable going along on that sort of guy's outing, whether it was good for business or not. And for some men, they may hate golf, beer, and of course the occasional strip club, but they do it anyway. We have different tools, and I learned this from a young analyst who worked for me several years ago. She used the male ego in a martial arts kind of way, using the power of the ego as leverage to get her male colleagues' attention. Though one time it did go just a tad too far (or rather, not far enough), as she wore the shortest leather dress I had ever seen for a meeting, and I made her go home and change. By the way, she also had one skirt that was made up entirely of men's neckties, sewn together lengthwise, as if each tie represented a conquest. I must say I got a kick out of it. She used her sexuality to great effect. She made men feel valued and admired. She reflected to them how they wanted to feel. And they were drawn to her. I watched and I learned. Flaunt it, have fun with it. Flirt, flatter.

Make it easy on yourself. As a young analyst, I learned to go where the men are. It's not exactly what you're thinking. I went to industries that few women chose to cover.

Run toward areas of your business where you're the only

woman rather than run away from them. As a young analyst, I could have gravitated to sectors that were considered more female friendly like retail or media, but instead I went after industrials and financials.

Part of the reason this is a good idea is that if you are a stock analyst covering Revlon or Polo, you will be one of many women in the room, but if you're covering John Deere or United Technologies, you get more CEO face time and possibly better intel. In real life, if you are a 7 out of 10 on the hotness scale, you're probably an 11 at a ball bearings convention. It's not even fair.

I also like to flirt in a very low-key way. I like to acknowledge the differences between men and women. It's fun. It doesn't kill you, and I think there is something electric and magnetizing about it. I think it's harmless, and if you are already attached, it makes you that much more attractive. I have one very big caveat: I would never flirt, in any way, with a man who works for me. There is a bright line that I don't want to go anywhere near. But a colleague—say, a guy on the show at CNBC—definitely. Or a guest on the show—absolutely. I've met a lot of famous, powerful men during their appearances on CNBC or elsewhere. I'm genuinely interested in hearing what they have to say. Some may find this flirtatious, and I play that up whenever I can. The CNBC team loves to put pictures of Jamie Dimon (the gruff, handsome CEO of JP Morgan) on the screen and then cut to me with animated hearts around my head. The truth is, I'm just a big talker. I am just as interested in the powerful women I meet—perhaps even more so—but it isn't flirtatious.

And let the men be men every once in a while. You don't need to insist they never hold the door open for you. Sometimes simple courtesy is too quickly judged as sexism. I trust that each woman has an internal compass to guide what feels right. At the risk of pissing off every feminist out there, I quote a classic line from Helen Gurley Brown, the famed, long-time editor of *Cosmopolitan*: "Sexual attention from men is almost always flattering." It's nice to be noticed, and it's nice to be appreciated. I don't think we need to banish courtliness.

The Finer Points

Eight Rules to Find Your Style and Look Your Best

"Nearly every glamorous, wealthy, successful career woman you might envy now started out as some kind of schlepp."

—Helen Gurley Brown

Me as an awkward twentysomething, and with a bit more fortysomething flair.

1. Find one signature style element (great shoes, great eye-glasses, short skirts, cropped hair) and run with it.

2. Buy multiples of anything you like, especially the non-designer-but-perfect-fitting things like favorite T-shirts. NOTE: I try to always have one to two unworn white T-shirts since they can make any outfit. And the corollary: Always have at least one white, crisp button-down shirt.

3. Keep your hair well cut, trimmed, and colored (if that's your thing).

4. Avoid "plain" at all costs—you will look 10 years older than you are.

5. If you are young, forget trying to look older—use it to your advantage.

6. Find the one store or designer that works for you—especially for key items. It will save you endless shopping grief. Make sure you know what looks good on you! I truly believe that investing two hours in a fashion consultant is a wise business move. For me, it's a sheath dress, made of luxurious fabric and expertly tailored, that shows some leg but isn't trying to turn my more boyish shape into an hourglass that isn't there, and a high, shapely heel.

7. Fashion designer Dana Buchman's advice from her mentor, Liz Claiborne—when you're dressing to go out, always take care with your hair, shoes, and handbag as well as your out-fit. So many women forget everything except the clothes. Beautiful scarf optional.

8. One last thought outside of work for women from the late, great author and director Nora Ephron:

"Oh, how I regret not having worn a bikini for the entire year I was twenty-six. If anyone young is reading this, go, right this minute, put on a bikini, and don't take it off until you're thirty-four." (In *I Feel Bad about My Neck: And Other Thoughts on Being a Woman*)

The Challenge of a First Job

Every successful career starts with a first job. Like my forays during what turned out to be two summers at CAA, first jobs are not usually spectacular and they are often full of disappointments, confusions, and tedium mixed in with moments of satisfaction and triumphs. Often that job can be mind-numbingly dull. But of course you've got to start somewhere, no matter where you plan on finishing. In this post–2008 meltdown economy, getting a job is far easier said than done. (This applies to midcareer jobs, too, where you may have to "settle" to get back in the door and use one experience to side-hop to your next big gig. First-job lessons can help us just as much when people wonder if we're overqualified and we can honestly say we're ready to learn, work hard, do what has to be done, and share the experience we do have, however it can be used.)

When I graduated from college in 1987, Wall Street firms couldn't hire enough young college graduates with a BS in Economics who knew absolutely nothing. (The BS part really shouldn't mean a Bachelor of Science.) In spite of my wallflower tendencies, I knew I was a member of a privileged crew. We were the toast of the town, or so we thought.

Times have changed dramatically, and those dreams of heading to big-name firms (in almost any field) are very hard to realize. In the business world today, you may be lucky to get any job. Financial pressures may force you to decide quickly and not risk a long, fruitless search for the perfect starter job. Even in the age of start-ups run by adolescents, you're unlikely to start anywhere near the top, or even at a level that you feel takes advantage of all your smarts and education. Most likely what you've got to offer are your wits, your attitude, and your work ethic, though probably in reverse order.

This reality may lead you to take any job you can get. That's OK. It's what you do with the job that's important. First jobs have so much to teach you. Think about it this way:

A first job is a chance to get paid to learn. So learn all you can.

You may have a misanthrope boss who is displeased by your mere presence. And there you have it—an instant lesson in how not to lead. You may be part of a team of over-worked, underpaid assistants who always need to be on call. There is a camaraderie in that bonding experience that can make for lifelong friendships. You can even learn about customer relations from a summer job scooping ice cream. But learn you must.

That's the key—learning. There's something there for you, if you pay attention and seek it out.

If you are a waitress, learn how a restaurant really runs. How do they make their money? Liquor? Special of the day? Turning over tables quickly? How does it work?

If you are an assistant to an ad exec at a magazine, ask, What's the most important division at a magazine and why?

Does the sales team seem to have the most influence or is the editorial group getting their way? And nothing beats the real-life learning about interpersonal skills you get from bartending. You will learn to sense who is looking to start a fight, show off, or just be a jerk and how to neutralize that. You'll become a good listener. These are skills that every successful CEO learned somewhere along the way.

Some of these first jobs are humbling and will forever be a measure for you to see how far you've come. It's a badge of honor for many, and it should be, to say, "I started as a _____."

Make it your business to learn as much as you can about the place where you're working. It's your job. You may even get paid to learn that you despise the industry you are in and you want to get out as quickly as you can. In this era, no one stays at her first job forever; it just doesn't work that way anymore.

Not every option you create is one you'll want to pursue, but you'll be surprised to discover the number of career experiences you're able to draw on in future positions. I always use the skill of thinking about what the agent would want next. It trained me to think one step ahead. Just asking myself what could happen next has been important in investing.

I have two specific caveats that must be highlighted. This is what I'll say to my daughters when they are in their early twenties and embarking on a career: "Don't lock yourself into something that really can't work for a 35-year-old woman and mother." This means if you ever want the possibility of a family and a home life, there are a few career paths to avoid.

Caveat #1: First of all, you *cannot* become an investment

banker—except for a very brief period of two to three years before you do something else (i.e., business school or, frankly, anything). You *must* have an exit plan. I mean it. Even if you follow all the tricks and lessons in the chapter "Let Yourself Off the Hook" so you *can* thrive at work and in life, this is a job where you are a neatly dressed indentured servant.

At the entry levels you are a glorified PowerPoint slave, albeit a decently paid one. You're putting together endless pitch books hoping to get retained by a company looking to do an acquisition or merger or other corporate transaction. My friend Brian from Wharton was horrified to learn that aside from being a Master-of-the-Universe-in-training and doing PowerPoint presentations, he would also be responsible for watering the plants. Not that there is anything wrong with watering the plants—it's just not how this future Master of the Universe pictured himself. Most of those pitch books end up being useless, but each one needs to be put together with the urgency of a Navy SEAL's mission to save the world from the apocalypse. And God forbid if there is a mistake in your Excel model. (This is actually a good lesson in checking and rechecking your work.)

Then, as a slightly more senior investment banker, you're only steps up the servitude ladder. You are then responsible for overseeing the neophyte bankers on how to do pitch books. And God forbid if there is a mistake in an Excel model. The servitude continues; you have no control over your schedule, and you are boot camp officer to the obnoxious 23-year-olds who cannot believe that they are not allowed in to high-level meetings. My friend Debbie knew it was the end when she had to get on a mandatory conference call to discuss an acquisition of a large education software company by an imperious CEO who eventually blew up her own company. Debbie missed her daughter waking up from a tonsillectomy. So her daughter woke up with no tonsils and Debbie had her heart ripped out. She is no longer an investment banker.

I know of only one woman who made it work at a very high level as an investment banker and a mother. One. She had an extremely hands-on husband who left his very challenging job at the highest echelons of consulting. Though they are both so type A, he eventually became a Harvard professor. They moved to Boston, and she commuted to New York.

So why are there no women running Wall Street firms?

Answer: There are almost no women running any big firms in *any* field. Wall Street is no different. You cannot be in charge of a family and run any big company. So you're down to women who don't have or want a family or are back in full force after launching a family, but not so far removed from the fray that they are not seen as not having the right stuff. (We'll see how Marissa Mayer does as CEO of Yahoo! where she made news taking the position when she was six months pregnant.) We are just now getting to a sufficient layer of women who have been working long enough to be chosen as CEO (i.e., those who are 50 or older, since they have to have been working since the early 1980s). That field narrows down to a very small number. It's just math.

Caveat #2: You cannot become a mergers and acquisitions corporate lawyer. You do not control your schedule, but rather you are at the beck and call of the senior partner who is in turn at the beck and call of the client. They really could not care less if you have weekend plans for Memorial Day.

It's an unwritten contract that corporate lawyers are on call for whatever client/deal/emergency/partner whim may arise.

This may not be any different than a surgeon or doctor who gets called in the middle of the night, but I imagine the psychic fulfillment from delivering a baby at 2 a.m. is far greater than making sure there is not a typo in a document at 2 a.m.

Whichever job you start with, whatever career North Star you're aiming for, you can't be certain at 22 that you will know what you want 10 or 20 years later. Even if you think you want to set the world on fire, I couldn't, in good conscience, encourage you or my daughters to be investment bankers or corporate lawyers. The road dead-ends at family life. You don't want to have to put yourself in a position where you don't have good options. You can waste a lot of energy bemoaning how unfair it is, but you wouldn't be particularly original. As Gloria Steinem put it in a line that has been widely quoted over the years, "I have yet to hear a man ask for advice on how to combine marriage and a career."

"Balance" is a comforting notion for women. Yes, men are doing more when it comes to raising children. But that's only part of the story. Many women won't give up some of the responsibilities for fear of not being seen as the perfect mother, even if no one else is watching them.

It gets much harder as you move down the career path, and then the other variables are thrown in the way. If you add in a life partner and/or kids, the right road to travel down may become less clear and, for women, harder to navigate.

As you start your career, and at turning points, consider this:

- Is this job "good enough" and a place where I can learn? Can I learn life skills even if I may leave this industry?
- Are there a few areas that tap into the things I naturally do well and am interested in? If I look at the job creatively, can I find those opportunities?
- What can I learn about this industry in general that could help me better understand the big picture?
- Thinking one or five steps ahead, can I imagine where I would go next?

Opening Doors

There really is no secret to success except working at it. Success is not linear. It can be stolen from you, lost, plateaued, and regained. But the experiences you gather, the wins you create, are yours for your whole life, and you can draw on them at every stage of your career. There are lots of ways to stay in the game and lots of lessons to learn. But if you begin by standing out, by taking the reins of your presence and visibility and abilities, you may open doors to opportunities that will last a lifetime.

CHAPTER 3

Build and Rebuild Momentum

To gain momentum, you need a push. Or several.

Here's the thing, though. There's no one to push you. You're on your own and you've got to push yourself. And you've got to find the people who will show you how. You do that by being proactive and not asking for permission.

I'm on the board of the Michael J. Fox Foundation for Parkinson's Research. I got involved 10 years ago because my mother-in-law, Sharon Golub, has been battling Parkinson's for years, but she's losing. She's one of the smartest, most insightful, intellectually curious, and kindest women I've ever known. Yet she's no match for this. You all know Michael Fox. Besides the energy, optimism, and extreme likability he brings to the cause, there's something else extraordinary about the Fox Foundation. If you were to ask, "Who's in charge of curing Parkinson's?" everyone involved with the Fox Foundation would say, "We are." Who gave them that mantle? No one. They just decided it and owned it. That perspective changes everything.

You need the confidence, or at least the gumption, to take on new challenges and responsibilities. You need the energy and hustle to make up for what you don't yet know. You need people around you to see your potential, to root for you, to help you steer yourself toward the best, right opportunities—even when you're full of doubts or wondering if you need to take three steps back before going one more step forward.

Who's responsible for making things happen? You are. Let this be your new perspective:

You are in charge of yourself, whether you like it or not.

Once you are off the predetermined life plan most of us start out with as kids—try hard, do well in high school, go to the best college you can—you're on your own. I remember one clear moment when I was a senior in college, walking across the campus green on a cold, brilliantly sunny end-of-winter day. The thought hit me and stopped me right in my tracks, literally. (Usually I keep walking, even during an aha moment. I'm just not that dramatic.) I realized, "I am the master of my destiny."

I was at the edge of the road map I had been following for so long. The well-worn path came to a dead stop, and folding out the next section of the map provided no route at all to follow. As Robert Frost would say, the path "in leaves no step had trodden black." For me, there would be no more asking for permission. I was the adventurer stepping into the wilderness. I was fully in charge.

It's impossible to know the trajectory of your career in advance. You may end up with a linear-looking path in a single company or industry with expected stepping-stones. You may end up job-hopping, boss-hopping, and industry-hopping till the various strands come together or one skill and passion get the upper hand and lead you to your most rewarding work. But when I look at the careers that have the most excitement, satisfaction, and rewards—financial and otherwise—the sense of movement and momentum is nearly universal. There are changes, new opportunities, and new challenges that pull people in those careers forward. An object in motion continues in motion, and an object at rest remains so.

You're not expected to have all the answers, especially early in your career, but you're expected to figure them out. Beginner or seasoned professional, you can't wait for the answers to come to you. If you're stalled or unhappy, you can't sit around and wait to gain momentum. You need to stake a claim to your career, your life, your decisions. That's what gives you the momentum you need. You need a mix of confidence and chutzpah (faux or otherwise), guides (mentors), and ambition (dreams). And you also need awareness (truth), so when you need to give yourself a boost, you recognize it and have the wherewithal to act.

Showing Confidence

As women, we aren't socialized to exude confidence. We aren't raised to be alpha males—neither the "alpha" part nor the "male" part. We're raised to get along well with others. In order to further that goal, even powerful women, the women who seem bold and firm and disarmingly independent, talk about their strong need to make those around them feel good and like they are being heard. Women love to discuss their challenges and problems. In the workplace, this is a mistake. We need to not just *appear* to be confident, but actually *be* confident.

One thing men do significantly better than women is convey confidence, even if it's misplaced or nonexistent. It seems as if confidence is hardwired into their psyches. They feel entitled to it, like it's a birthright.

I see this all the time in the investing business and even more on television among the various traders on CNBC. Men feel comfortable saying things with certainty, without hesitation, even if they can't possibly know how things will play out. No one can predict what the stock market is going to do from one day to the next, yet there are plenty of male market commentators who talk with such certainty they make it seem like you're an idiot if you don't concur with the genius of their opinion.

At the hedge fund I run, Metropolitan Capital Advisors, LP, we manage money for high–net worth individuals, families, institutions, and banks. I need to confidently lead our team and project confidence to our investors in every communication I have with them. Even though I have no idea what's going to come next in the market, I need to convey that I have the intellect and the skills to manage through it. I tell them that in my 25 years of experience, I've seen all kinds of markets, from panic to euphoria and exuberance to despair, but those are just human reactions, not true arbiters of the value of companies and business models. Our strategy at Metropolitan is to focus on what is known as "value." It sounds vague, but what it means in the Wall Street lexicon is companies that trade at a discount to inherent measures of true net worth. We're looking for underdogs, unsung heroes, companies that others have underestimated. Companies become value investments because they may be out of favor at the moment, or there has been some disruption in their business that the market doesn't know how to interpret.

For example, a property and casualty insurance company right after Hurricane Sandy or banks and home builders in the wake of the 2008 financial collapse and recession of 2009 may find their companies' stock and even their whole industries' valuations reduced to mere fractions of their true net worth. My team of analysts and I try to build a portfolio of excellent risk/reward positions. We look for companies in industries where we believe in the underlying value, even if it is not being fully realized in the moment. We try to assess what we can make if we're right, what we can lose if we're wrong, and if there is a way to hedge some of the downside risk. It is worth noting that I am the largest individual investor in our fund, so I care very deeply about our portfolio. It's a persuasive selling point that I have enough confidence in what we do that I am willing to put the bulk of my net worth in our funds.

My firm has one big difference from almost every other hedge fund in existence. Five of the top six positions are held by women. This is by design. Let me tell you why.

A friend of mine who runs a hedge fund has no women analysts working for him. (I have always had women analysts.) When I asked him why not, he gave me this very candid answer. "Men come in with ideas and pound the table and tell me how much money we can make. Women come in and tell me all the ways the investment could go wrong. Since I only have a limited amount of capital to invest I'm going to listen to the one with the most conviction, the most confidence, every time." He's not the only person who thinks like that.

For me, when analysts walk into my office with a pound-the-table idea and very strong conviction, one of my first questions for them is, "What's the downside? What could go wrong?" If they don't have good answers to these questions, they haven't done a good job analyzing the situation. I see that they haven't broken down the decision and haven't identified the risks. They can't just show me the scenario where everything goes right. I have to be able to understand what could go wrong also. It's only with a full picture that one can make good decisions.

I recognize this approach doesn't make for a "wow" pitch. I consciously try not to let women's and my staff's more tempered, cautious style cloud the process of my weighing the pros and cons and keep me from jumping on an opportunity because the enthusiasm for it is measured. I recognize that they might not present their confidence in a recommendation in a way that is always obvious.

Sometimes, though, the one-sided "wow" pitch is in order, especially if you are pitching men.

So this one time I offer this advice with a "do as I say, not as I do" philosophy. There are times we women need to abandon our more measured risk-averse comfort zone and put ourselves out there with table-pounding confidence. And as we say on the show *Fast Money*, it makes for better TV. Know whom you're pitching.

If you're struggling with this concept and think that the

"facts should speak for themselves" or that "I don't want to be a phony" or "I hate playing the game and selling and pitching my boss and the higher-ups," here's some food for thought: Even leaders like to be led. Many women are afraid to take the risk of being on the line for the success or failure of a particular call. In investing, if the position fails, and they have laid out all the risks beforehand, they can pin it on the portfolio manager (who actually gives the go-ahead to buy a position) by rationalizing, "Well, I laid out the downside and they chose to go ahead anyway."

The more money analysts make for us, the more power they get by getting capital allocated to their ideas. And they can't make money for us if we don't give their ideas a chance. But if we want the success, the excitement, and power that come with running a division or being in a position of power, we don't have the luxury of never taking risks. Men don't have it; why should we?

I need people who have the confidence to disagree, who don't hesitate to respectfully tell me why they think I'm wrong. I love the confidence of someone who can do that. This is why being able to assert yourself is a key for success whether you're at the beginning of your career or the newly minted boss.

Ways to show confidence and conviction:

- Always do your homework—whether for new processes, new business, or recommendations of any sort. Think of your pitch as if you're in a debate club and you've been assigned the side of telling why your idea is a great one. Let the other side worry about poking holes in the idea;

you don't need to do it for them. But you better know the downside and be ready to answer questions about it. Just don't say it up front.

- Present your case as succinctly, clearly, and tactfully as possible right at the top. Start with the punch line but be prepared to offer significant backup. Even if a different decision is made than the one you recommend, your work is noticed and usually respected.
- Avoid piecemeal information at all costs. It creates a muddle and will make people work harder—that saps momentum rather than adding to it.

Faking It Wisely

One of the most important things I've learned about momentum is that there are times when you have to act "as if" you're at the place you want to be. There are times when you're going to feel as if you are faking it, that you don't know what you're doing and you're a fraud. The inside joke of it all is that everyone feels like that at some time. And it's OK. What is faux at first will become real after practice. As a parent, a boss, a working person out in the world, as a grown-up, sometimes you just have to fake it.

There is not necessarily a singular moment when your expertise is established. It gets built slowly over time, experience by experience, from success and failure both. I remember my inaugural trip to our pediatrician with my first set of twins, Lucy and Jack, who were just two weeks old at the time. I was filling out the necessary forms and came upon the question "Mother's Place of Birth," and I thought, "Where was my mother born?" Then it hit me—I was the mother! So I had better start thinking of myself as somebody's mother, whether I believed I was ready or not. Confidence is often faked before it's earned. Ironically, the truth is this:

Women think they are faking it when they're not, because most women never feel they are ready.

I remember the first time, as a full-fledged grown-up working person, I had the courage to speak up on my behalf on a big issue with confidence—even with doubts below the surface. It was at my first post–college graduation job. I lived alone in a one-bedroom apartment in the 60s on the Upper East Side of New York. It was big for just me, and I decorated it using money from graduation gifts and searched for some things from ABC, the chic furniture store from which I thought I would buy everything but could actually only afford a rug—nothing on top of it.

Jeffrey Schwarz, my lifelong friend and work partner, offered me the opportunity to work with him setting up a new risk arbitrage fund for the Belzberg family. They were high-flying Canadian financiers, meaning they made bids for companies they believed were worth significantly more than what the market was reflecting. It was my dream job, literally, doing exactly what I thought I was destined to do. We were in the fanciest of fancy office buildings on the corner of Park Avenue and 59th Street. It was a black glass tower worthy of an office for Gordon Gekko. The marble-clad floor exuded power and cool aloofness that, ironically, I was excited to step foot on every day. This was the roaring '80s and takeover deals were a daily occurrence. The Wall Street machine of bankers, lawyers, stock traders, brokers, and ru- mormongers was operating on all cylinders. The bigger the deals, the better.

The Belzbergs knew Jeffrey, who was the wunderkind from a large fund called Kellner DiLeo, one of the biggest risk arbitrage firms on the Street. The firm made huge re- turns (i.e., tens of millions of dollars) from the mid '70s to the late '80s on hundreds of takeover deals. Jeffrey was the twentysomething young star freshly minted from Wharton. Based on his success at Kellner DiLeo, these Canadian bil- lionaires decided to give him $30 million to run in 1987 and anointed him as the head of their new risk arbitrage invest- ment fund. This was considered a very large start-up at that time. They wanted Jeffrey to build an organization that fo- cused on stocks that were involved in takeovers.

This strategy is known as risk arbitrage. An example: Company X receives a takeover bid from Company Y. A risk arbitrageur may buy Company X and hope to make the spread between the price he buys the shares for and the price that Company Y (or some other company) will ultimately pay for it. That spread is known as the arbitrage. However, many times deals fall apart for all kinds of reasons, includ- ing that Company X might not want to sell itself. It may reject the bid and Company Y may then withdraw its bid and go away. Company X's stock would then fall back near the price it was before Company Y ever made the bid—that loss you would incur as a shareholder is the "risk" part of risk arbitrage.

Jeffrey was clearly in his element, groomed for just such a job. I, on the other hand, was fresh from Wharton and knew next to nothing except what I had learned in my finance courses, including my favorite class, Options and Speculative Markets, or Fin 6 as we called it. But he hired me because he needed someone willing to work like crazy doing all the grunt work necessary (a total beginner) but who also had an interest in learning this rather arcane area of the business (when most people arriving on Wall Street would want to start at a top white shoe firm in the trading, corporate finance, or investment banking departments). The timing was perfect for both of us.

It was my luck that Jeffrey actually knew me through my sister Wendy. They were close friends at Wharton (before she went to Hollywood), and we all spent Thanksgiving breaks near each other in Boca Raton, Florida, when I was still in high school. As a 16-year-old tomboy, I would play football on the beach with Jeffrey and ask him about his work as a risk arbitrageur. He was the only real-life one I knew.

I started out working for Jeffrey as a trader, mainly executing buy-and-sell orders according to direction set by Jeffrey and the research department, but I was also learning the business. Partway into my second year, I realized that research was a more valuable skill set. The research group figures out what could go wrong in the deal, what the merger agreement between the buyer and seller provides for and protects against, and what regulatory hurdles there are to getting a deal done. Just as importantly, they also try to figure out what companies are really worth based on a number of factors such as how much cash flow they generate and what their competitive position is in the industry. They may make educated guesses as to which other companies or private equity firms could also be bidders for a given company. The work of this role generated far more value than the trading side. In the grand scheme of investing, I realized I needed to understand what companies were worth and why. If I headed down the trading path too long, I would get stuck there. My map showed a dead end on this path, though it was off in the distance.

I knew I had to make the switch to research, and Jeffrey was close to hiring someone for just such a position. Fortunately, Jeffrey had taken great interest in my career development, and we would talk about it often. During one of those talks, I told him that I really wanted the shot at the job. I told him I had concluded I needed to switch to research from trading. He said I could do both. I told him that I believed he *thought* that was better for me but it wasn't and to please not hire someone else.

Just voicing that desire to prevent the hire of a new research analyst was extremely proactive for me, but I had to show him he should consider me for that new position. To prove that I was ready to make the transition to the research side, I had to show both him and myself that I could make the shift to thinking about things differently—to considering all the elements of a deal, not just the technical or math side of analyzing the stocks we might trade in. A few weeks after we had that conversation, I showed that shift with one emphatic recommendation I made.

Federated Department Stores, which owned a host of storied retailers such as Jordan Marsh, Burdines, Wanamaker's, Dayton's, Marshall Field's, and Bloomingdale's, received a takeover bid from Allied Stores for $47 a share in January 1988. Without having the skills to do the research, I still came to the conclusion that we really needed to own Federated stock and options, and here's why:

Federated was a unique property, and intuitively I knew there would always be someone out there, some ego-driven investor—always a man, in my experience—who needs to own these big, flashy, famous iconic properties. Someone was going to pay more for it, I reasoned. What says "I have arrived" better than owning the iconic Bloomingdale's in the heart of Manhattan, a retailing jewel akin to the Hope Diamond?

Without even having an understanding of its cash flow or of what kind of financing would be available to potential buyers, I knew in my gut that someone would "need" to own it at any price. Luckily, here was a situation where financial modeling (that I didn't yet do well) wasn't the critical piece to understanding the opportunity. I "pounded the table" with my emphatic conviction that we needed to own a position in Federated. I don't know if Jeffrey listened to me to be kind, to be humoring, because he was going to own the stock anyway, or because I convinced him, but we bought a lot of Federated.

Sure enough, a bidding war ensued with multiple egos (oops, I mean bidders) entering the fray. Ultimately Robert Campeau (head of Allied stores) ended up paying a *huge* price for Federated, and we made millions. It was my first big stock recommendation, and my quasi/faux confidence in myself was replaced with a little bit of actual confidence on which I could build. I had never before heard the term *trophy property*, but I sensed the meaning.

I have a long-standing philosophy now that I employ on appropriate occasions: Trophy properties *always* get sold, in *any* market. This means that if a unique high-profile asset is for sale, it doesn't matter what the state of the world or financial markets is, someone will step up to buy it and either pay a full price or a ridiculous price, but it will get sold. And it doesn't matter if the deal makes financial sense, whether it's a sports team or Pebble Beach or the Plaza Hotel. (As an interesting aside, Campeau's ego did him in. He paid too much for Federated as the economy went into a recession in 1989, and it bankrupted him.)

Unfortunately, that same recession brought an end to the era of the big deals and leveraged buyouts. Just as I was on my way to becoming a research analyst with one big victory under my belt, Wall Street's deal-making machine collapsed and the Belzberg fortune collapsed with it, forcing them to close down the fund. I wouldn't learn the research side of the business there. I would have to make another move to gain momentum somewhere else. I would need to convince someone else to hire me.

Ideas for faking it wisely:

- Learn everything you can about your potential boss. Everyone likes to talk about themselves.
- Learn everything you can about the industry from all the information that's out there. Don't wait for knowledge to come to you.
- Ask questions to someone you trust. Be judicious in asking questions that may reveal your naiveté if you can ask later. There is a phrase in bank analysis called Other Real Estate Owned whose acronym is OREO. When I laughed at the acronym as I was asking what it meant, I was outed as a neophyte.

Doubt the Doubts

Our career paths aren't always linear. Every time we need to make a change, it takes a lot of energy and nerve. It takes invention and reinvention. Yet as hard as the change is, it's better than the alternative, which is being stuck and waiting. You can bemoan it and wish all the opportunities coming to others were coming to you, or you can regroup. As I always remind myself and my children, life is not a contest to see how well you can live someone else's life. It's about living your own.

The notion of the 30-year career at one place is beyond passé, but I didn't know it then, and there are still lots of people who feel that a career path should be laid out for them even if they see it's the exception rather than the rule. I certainly didn't accept the reality that change was inevitable when I was in my 20s.

At 25, my future looked bleak. Could my career really be over already? I thought to myself. I was filled with self-doubt. I would need to marshal all my nerve again to try to find a job in research at some other risk arbitrage fund during a time when Wall Street was in a dizzying decline. My secret identity of not being a research analyst was sure to be unmasked as soon as I landed my first interview.

I got a few leads from friends and associates and went out to fake my way into a research job. Honestly, it was as if I were auditioning for the role of research analyst, because I really wasn't one.

I got in the door at a few places, some where I clearly didn't belong or want to belong even if they would have me, one where I felt I wouldn't be challenged enough because they wanted me to focus on trading, and one that was such a mismatch as I had none of the skills they needed and they had no use for any of the skills I did have. It was the business interview equivalent of a blind date where a dog-loving guy asks the girl if she likes dogs and she responds that she's horribly allergic and was bitten by a German shepherd as a child. I was getting very nervous as I only had $6,000 to my name. And in a stroke of financial-planning genius, I thought it would be fine to spend $1,500 on a Shaker antique desk that I really wanted (and didn't negotiate over because I hate conflict and was too naive to know you could negotiate), so then I was down to $4,500. I had to keep going though. As one woman executive I know has taped to her computer, "Doubt your doubts."

Then one interview felt just right. In fact, I interviewed a few times at Donaldson, Lufkin, Jenrette (DLJ), a big, venerable Wall Street firm that had built itself up from nothing to be a force in investment banking, trading, and industry research. It was a breeding ground for some of Wall Street's next generation of stars, such as Tony James, who now is the president of Blackstone. DLJ chose Chris Flynn for its new head of risk arbitrage.

Chris was the quirky-but-cool, prematurely gray-haired workaholic who was plucked from Guy Wyser-Pratte's eponymous firm. In the risk arbitrage arena at that time, Guy Wyser-Pratte was synonymous with Ivan Boesky, minus the insider trading. In fact, Wyser-Pratte's book, with the flairless title *Risk Arbitrage*, was required reading for anyone in the risk arb business. I loved it. I may have been the only one.

To get ready for the interview, I studied all the deals happening at the time and fortunately knew the answers to Chris's questions. I was thrilled when he made me an offer for even more money than I had been making. We hit it off personally as well, and I enjoyed his funky style. He had very cool catlike glasses, and he constantly ran his fingers through his long, hip gray hair to brush it back from his eyes. He liked practical jokes, and while I was afraid of him at first, I soon realized he really wanted to be liked. Chris and our team would talk about art and movies and then debate the best choice for that day's lunch. He had a very pretty, funny wife, Wendy, and they loved to tell stories of Wendy's parents' dismay at her not having married a Jewish guy. I had landed in a safe place.

To my supreme good fortune, Chris spoon-fed me the business the way *he* wanted me to do it. He thought I was being a really good sport when I didn't bristle under his exacting direction and didn't insist on doing tasks my way. (Little did he know, I didn't know a "my way," or really *any* way.) I, on the other hand, figured it was my graduate course in research. I learned fast, and I had some things that I could teach him as well. (That's a big thing that young people forget—as do more experienced people as well. We always bring life experience to our work that isn't replaceable. Everyone has unique knowledge to contribute if we're curious *and* proactive.)

I was very conversant with the nascent world of options. Options, which come in two basic flavors called either "puts" or "calls," are securities investors can use to make risky bets or, counterintuitively, to help hedge their risk. For example, buying a call gives the owner the right, but not the obligation, to buy a stock at a preset price (called the strike price) until a certain date (called the expiration date). Options can allow you to control big positions in stocks while only putting up a portion of the money to control such a position, and to precisely know your risk.

For example, a call option for IBM struck at $200/share for two months from now may cost $10. So you could control shares for $10/share instead of paying $200/share. However, two months from now, the call will expire, so if the stock is below $200, you lose the $10 you put up, but you can only lose $10 maximum, even if the stock went to, say, $150 or lower. That is the risk management use of an option. You know exactly how much you can lose (the $10 you put up); with the stock itself, you never know with precision. If the stock is above $200 a share, you need to "exercise" and put up the $200 a share. At the expiration date, your ability for leverage will expire. Most risk arbitrage firms were not familiar with options then, so I clearly had added value there. I could lead the group in this one small area, even when I still was a beginner in so many others. In fact, with the speed of change in business today, there's almost always someone who can take a leadership role on some new development. I was finding my stride there, enjoying the work and feeling like I wasn't really faking it anymore.

Interestingly, since Chris was stolen away from a large risk arbitrage firm to head the DLJ team, his ex-boss, Guy Wyser-Pratte, tried to hire me for more money to be their option expert as a way to get back at Chris. But I preferred Chris. I could just sense that even though Wyser-Pratte was willing to pay me more, he wouldn't respect me the way Chris did, and I wouldn't have a strong role in the firm.

Sometimes, though, it's still flattering to be asked to dance, even if you don't like the guy. Turning down more money was easily the right thing to do at that moment. It wasn't even close.

Midway through 1992, though, I realized the risk arbitrage business was significantly altered and wouldn't return to its former glory for a while, if ever. I could see that no matter how good a risk arbitrageur you were, you were stuck in a sector that wasn't offering any opportunities. My momentum with Chris and risk arbitrage, in its then form, had run its course. However, I did have transferable skills. I knew how to value companies. That would be tremendously useful. Once again, I would need to change course. I was at an impasse; I needed to back up and go around. Joanna Coles, *Cosmopolitan* editor, recently shared with me this piece of advice that I wish I had much earlier: "Don't expect a job to be open-ended or last forever. Have a plan for where what you are doing right now is leading."

Reluctantly, I knew that it was time to move on.

Jeffrey, who had been both my boss and mentor, and I conjured up a plan that would have me become his partner—albeit junior partner, but partner nonetheless—in setting up a hedge fund, though he had solidified the role of mentor for me and would continue in that position as well. It would be less of everything that I had at DLJ—less money, less prestige, less infrastructure, less camaraderie with a big group. Joanna Coles also tells how twice she's taken pay cuts for opportunities, and it's always worked out. Even though it was going backwards, in the end it would lead me forward.

When momentum seems stalled and you're stagnating, or

feel like other people are getting ahead, you need to step back and look at the map overall. It's so easy to get lost in the details of doing a good job, and if you've hit a snag, keeping your nose to the grindstone can seem safe. But you can look at things another way. Getting very focused on the few important and big things on your plate can have a major impact.

If you honestly conclude you are on the right path, rocky though it may be—because no path is entirely smooth and downhill—then set some tangible goals to gain momentum. Imagine meeting one or two important people inside or outside your organization; bringing in one new client or relationship important to your division; or having one clear, executable idea that would have an immediate financial return (in revenue or cost savings). Make meeting the goals your job. Fold up the map and move forward.

Guidelines for assessing the timing and need to change:

- Look at the cause of the stalled momentum. Is it you, or is it your industry, your role in it, or your particular organization? Answer that question with the most untainted eye that you can.
- If you were just entering the workforce right now, is the path you are on the one you would take? How many of us haven't had to look deeply at our current significant other and ask ourselves, "Is this really the one I should be with?" From somewhere inside yourself, if you're honest, the answers will come to you.

Seek a Mentor

A mentor is not imperative to success; it's just helpful—hugely helpful. A mentor is someone who can guide you in your career by giving you a perspective that you wouldn't otherwise have. It's someone who knows the industry and the players and understands the bigger picture. It's also someone who can assess your strengths and weaknesses and tell you what you need to work on. They are part teacher, part coach, part agent or manager, and part friend or parent—a parent who cares less about you than your mother but knows a lot more about your industry. A mentor can explain the hierarchy of the business, sometimes shedding light on an undercurrent that might not be immediately recognizable.

Early on, when I was learning how takeover deals really worked, I listened carefully to each constituency: The bankers for Bidders A claimed there were no others interested, so they shouldn't have to pay more to acquire Company B. Bankers for Company A described their bid as "full and fair." But what Jeffrey soon taught me was that the language was code from Company A. So I had to filter each piece of information through the lens of "how this is helping them" and not taking every statement at face value. I needed someone to teach me this lesson. Look at the information you're getting through the lens of the teller. "What's in it for him?" In the takeover business, "full and fair" means, "We're not going to pay more either until someone else comes in willing to pay more, or Company B shows us why it is so valuable by allowing us to see confidential information—then we'll pay more." Well, that sure is different from what I thought "our bid is full and fair" meant. It is tremendously helpful to have someone who can explain the big picture of the business you're in. I needed to understand that in life and in business things are often not what they seem.

Sometimes, for a woman, if you get taken under the wing of a high-profile man, people will talk. I used to worry that people would think Jeffrey and I were having an affair. I knew we weren't, and he knew we weren't, but people wondered. They'll talk in a good way and a bad way. It doesn't matter; you can't worry about it.

My friend in the book business had a mentor who showed her the ropes in the business—what worked, what didn't, what made one book successful over another one that may be just as good. She eagerly absorbed this time, attention, and expertise. She knew it bred some resentment among the ranks, but it was such valuable advice—she was happy to take it. And people will also take a second look at you if they see that someone else has found you worthy of their effort to help you along in your career. Hey, if someone else wants you, there must be something worthy, right? Watch two babies each with a toy playing next to each other. Soon enough, each one will covet the other's toy. It's human nature, and it doesn't change when you grow up.

There are three simple truths of mentor relationships I always share with people:

- Like all important relationships, a connection with a mentor does not happen overnight. It's not a job description or an assigned role. (And if you *are* assigned a mentor at your company, take advantage of the program and person, learn all you can, but don't think it's a replacement for the true investment and caring that the right mentor relationship can bring.)

- A mentor is investing in you just as you are investing in them. The relationship evolves over time.
- You and your mentor are making a bet on each other. You want and need each other to succeed.

How to choose a mentor: The best man for the job may be a man

1. Start where you are and choose someone you have access to. If it's your very first job, just being able to ask someone who's been there even a year could be helpful enough. Looking down shouldn't be ruled out either. Personal assistants and secretaries can offer an excellent lay of the land, particularly when it comes to reading the needs of the bosses. For example, they may advise, "Never ask to speak to the boss if the door is closed; it means she is in a terrible mood."

2. Think about choosing a man. Most women feel a kinship with other women and welcome the help of a maternal figure. So naturally that would lead you to seek a woman mentor. That natural inclination is generally a mistake. Why such a rule today? If you're headed to a male-dominated field like Wall Street, real estate development, or politics, the reality is you're going to find more senior men than you are women. Don't make it about sexuality; it's just math.

3. Pick a man who has daughters—he'll see them in you and want to help.

4. Do not choose an unmarried middle-aged woman

with no family. If you have or want to have a family, this is not your best bet. She may very well be more devoted and capable of putting more time and energy into the job than you may be able to match. A tension will invariably arise. And you must be prepared to outwork your mentor.

5. Look backwards—someone from your last job (depending on the circumstances of how you left), maybe even your boss, may be able to give you some great perspective.

6. You don't necessarily need to propose with, "Will you be my mentor?" That could be seen as somewhat forced and calculating, especially if it's a bit premature. Instead, approach them after you've been there for a while and tried to absorb as much as you could and you get to an important milestone, such as your first job review. That might be a good time to seek counsel on how to handle it.

If you're the mentor yourself, in the corporate world there is no shame in expecting something back when you give of yourself and your resources. By picking a good mentee, you can gain a valuable player for your team. On occasion, it becomes apparent that you have a superstar on your hands. Be prepared for the day when the superstar outgrows you and the relationship. That's OK. Help in their trajectory; it won't reflect poorly on you. And they could become invaluable while you're helping them.

My girlfriend Juli had a superstar assistant, Nancy, randomly assigned to her when she was an editor of a magazine section. Nancy did everything, anticipated every need, rewrote copy, and got coffee, always with an upbeat attitude but not too sunny a disposition (perfect for Juli).

Juli heard about a job opening for an assistant editor role at another magazine at the parent company. Even though she hated the idea of losing Nancy, she knew she didn't want to get in Nancy's way. It would have been easy for Juli to keep mum about the position without Nancy ever knowing about the missed opportunity, but that's not the way Juli operates. She knew she could make do without her. Juli wholeheartedly recommended Nancy, who got the job, and years later, when Nancy became the editor of that sister magazine and Juli needed freelance work while she was home with her children, I'm sure you can guess who gave it to her.

The Finer Points

The Travel Cheat Sheet for Mentees and Everyone Aspiring to Succeed

(Profoundly obvious and somewhat obscure tips to make the most of your travel opportunity)

1. Never have anyone else carry your luggage. Pack only what you can easily manage.

2. Make sure your suitcase is in good working order.

3. Make sure you know backup routes to your destinations (lodging, meeting place, and airports, etc.). Check for any construction projects / parades / etc. that may alter the travel route. Have these directions printed and accessible. Do not rely solely on GPS. (NOTE: Tip #3 applies whether

you're the designated junior person or part of the lead team. Everyone responds to a calm guide in the storms of travel.)

4. Be prepared to do the driving and offer (particularly if you are a good driver).

5. If your boss loves Starbucks, brownies, BBQ, or some local specialty, know the location of a few standouts.

6. Never, never be the last one ready.

7. Have extra printed copies of your presentation easily accessible and be sure the presentation is also saved on your computer.

8. No matter what snags you encounter, never, never complain.

I can't convey enough to you how well it reflects on you to anticipate what may be needed and to be prepared for the unexpected. You will make yourself invaluable, even if your skills may be somewhat subpar in other areas. You can work on those skills over time. Some skills you already possess—you just need to be thinking one step ahead. This is a theme I will return to over and over. Ask yourself what comes next or what could possibly come next. You will appear to be very smart.

To Really Gain Momentum, Find a Great Boss

A corollary to finding a great mentor is finding a great boss. However, most often you really don't have much say in that. But every once in a while, you get a chance to work on something with someone you admire or maybe are slightly even in awe of. Try to gain as much access to them as you can. Try to get on a project that they are heading, even if you have to ask to be placed on it. Or even volunteer yourself to help if you haven't been chosen for an official role. Then, quite obviously, you need to work your tail off. Help the project succeed in any way you can. Always be fully prepared for every meeting.

A chance to travel with that person is a big, big opportunity. You can show some other skills since travel can be a metaphor for life. What you ultimately learn is often not about the specific project or investment or client. Maybe there are some tricks of the trade or lingo to learn. But really it's about two things. First, it's about how to think—how to learn the discipline of thinking so you can really understand the business. And in leadership, it's about character. That's what I remember and what I try to convey. I knew I was better off working with Chris for less money than with someone else for whom I had no respect. I've seen some very poor behavior in my day. Phone slamming, screaming, belittling, demeaning—but I mostly saw that as voyeur and not as a direct report to such bosses. Those histrionics stick with you and can't be erased. (Remember that if you become a boss.) I've also had the privilege of witnessing grace, generosity, brilliance, wisdom, and an intense work ethic, which will not be forgotten.

Here are a few truths about people I've learned by observation and experience:

- People sometimes do stupid things—sometimes that's the only explanation there is. There isn't a hidden "crazy like a fox" underlying reason; it's just really stupid.

- People lie—if you are a truthful person, you will find this hard to believe.
- People trust other people in direct proportion to the amount they themselves can be trusted.
- People have reasons that are not always clear, obvious, or the same as ours. Always ask yourself what the other person's motivation is—what do they want to get out of this exchange? How or why are they spinning the information they're giving you?
- There are people motivated by kindness directly from their heart. Accept it. Try to share it. And be aware that they are far, far less likely to be wealthy and powerful.

If you're struggling with a "bad" boss—if they are truly "bad"—figure out how you can get out as soon as possible. Do these things if you possibly can: save money, have a security fund, let people know you're looking to make a move. Toxic bosses don't get better. You can sometimes outlast a bad boss, and it can be worth staying for a reasonable amount of time if you continue learning, building your knowledge and visibility, and finding some enjoyment, perhaps with colleagues. But a boss that stalls you personally will squash your momentum and sap you for a very long time.

My friend Dana Buchman told me of how she job-hopped many times, working for one (fill in profane adjective followed by profane noun) after another. If they wouldn't pay her fairly, she quit. If they were exceedingly disrespectful, she quit. If they wanted sexual favors, she quit. She just kept quitting—more than half a dozen times—until she found the place and people she loved working for: Liz Claiborne and Art Ortenberg. So right was the place, so "open and joyful" and wonderful were Liz and Art that Dana stayed for 26 years until she retired.

Always Think Ahead

You can start with the simplest skills to make an impact and get the help you need to get ahead. The most obvious things you do can be the most important—and, shockingly, the most overlooked.

Dana tells the story of the president of the Dana Buchman division in the mid-80s meeting with Art Ortenberg. She was in the room when he, the division president, didn't have an answer that Art had expected him to have because a person hadn't gotten back to him. Art's advice was succinct and visual: He held up his finger and said, "See that? That's a finger." He then pointed with the same finger to the telephone sitting on the desk. "See that? That's a telephone."

Dana always remembered Art's advice and translates it three ways:

1. If email doesn't work, call—personal contact usually will get you the answer.

2. There's often a way to get info that you may not be in the habit of turning to. It's not necessarily the first thing that comes to mind.

3. Often it's too easy to blame someone else, as in [whine], "I couldn't get the info because he didn't get back to me." If that thought pops up in your mind, use it as a trigger for this "finger to the telephone" image and come up with a more direct/creative alternative way to get the info.

At CNBC, we have a page program, and every six weeks a new page rotates onto the *Fast Money* set. One of their responsibilities is to get each of us, the panelists, to sign a disclosure form showing which stock positions we have. Early in my tenure on the show, we had a lovely young page who, each day, would say, "Miss Finerman, could you please fill out this disclosure form?" I would respond, "Sure. Do you have a pen?" And she would say, "Oh, I'll go get one."

This went on every day for six weeks. (I realize I could have brought my own pen and I almost always carry one, but I was testing her. Yes, people really get tested.) Finally, on the last day of her internship, she handed me the form with the usual, "Miss Finerman, will you please fill this out?" Before I could ask her for a pen, she smiled, very knowingly and self-satisfied, and said, "You need a pen, don't you?" I said, "Yes," and she responded, "Oh, OK. I'll go get you one." Sweet personality, but always 10 yards behind, not one step ahead. (If someone ever moved her cheese, she'd be dead in a week.)

The next Monday, a new page introduced himself and said, "Miss Finerman, could you please fill out this form?" I said, "Sure. Do you have a pen?" He went to go get one. Tuesday, the same thing: "Miss Finerman, could you please fill this out?" My turn: "Sure, but I need a—" and before I could say "pen," he held out his hands, palms up, with a pen in each. "Blue or black?" he asked. I may not remember any other task he performed during his rotation with us, but I promise you, if he called me today and asked me for help, I would help him. We use the phrase all the time on the set to describe someone who gets it: "Blue or black."

Blue or black—it may be the beginner version, but the lesson of this message is relevant for our entire careers. Always think one step ahead. The best risk arbitrageurs don't just think about what is likely to come next; they think about what the market's reaction may be and then what will come after that. And the best value investors delight in a market panic, knowing that that is the time to buy. They don't think about the moment right in front of them; they think well beyond that.

CHAPTER 4

Take Asymmetric Risks

Asymmetric risk is a term we use in investing that basically means a risk where the magnitude and likelihood of one outcome—say, the upside (the reward)—is much greater than the magnitude and likelihood of the other outcome: say, the downside (risk). Let's say you get invited to a cocktail party where you don't know anyone. This opportunity presents an asymmetric risk. You may have a bad time, in which case you can just leave (the loss is small). Or you may meet some great people who become lifelong friends or just provide for an entertaining evening, or one of them may be the person of your dreams (the reward could be quite large).

Looking at risk this way can make it much easier to stretch ourselves in new situations and opportunities—our logical minds can see just how small the downside is of doing something we may really resist—especially the shy and introverted among us. Often it's only the downside that we see, so we decline things without giving one moment's consideration to the possible upside.

Let me give you an example of an asymmetrical trade I made 24 years ago. It was at my first job on Wall Street, and

I was working on a complicated stock and options trade. It's not worth going too deep into the weeds, but here's the gist.

What's the Worst that Could Happen?

We owned shares of United Airlines (UAL), which agreed to be taken over in a leveraged buyout (LBO) by a group of investors, just as many other companies had agreed to do that year, like RJR Nabisco and Revco drugstores. In an LBO, an investor or group of investors buy all the shares of a company at a premium and becomes the new owner. Typically, the buyers finance the purchase of the company with mostly borrowed money—which is the "leverage" in a leveraged buyout. The new owners have a stake of their own money in the company and the borrowed money, which eventually will need to be paid back.

The idea is that the new owners then seek to improve management and productivity to eke out more profit and, even more importantly, to pay back the borrowed funds like someone who has a mortgage on a house. After all the borrowed money is paid off, the new owners have 100 percent ownership of the company. The returns on these kinds of investments can be staggeringly high, but they are not without risk.

Meanwhile, the deal is attractive to the current owners because they are selling their company, often through their stock ownership, at a price well above the current value of the company. RJR Nabisco was trading below $75 per share before KKR ultimately paid stockholders $109 per share to take them private. In the UAL deal, the buyers were going to pay $300 per share for all the shares with money borrowed from Japanese banks and thereby gain control of the company. A bidding war had taken the stock from the mid-$150s per share in August 1989 to nearly $300 per share, which was being offered to shareholders by a group including UAL employees and private equity. Some financing and regulatory obstacles remained before the $300 deal could close, so the shares were trading at $280 per share as the shareholders awaited the closing of the deal. Thus, we stood to make $20 for each share we owned.

I had an idea, though. I devised a strategy to "hedge" our position—that is, to make money if the stock went down a little. Analyzing the situation, I thought there was about a 15 percent chance that the stock could drop to $260 a share if there was a delay in the closing of the deal. In such a scenario, our option trade—called a "1x2 put spread" for the traders among you—would go from being worth the $2.62 a share that it cost to purchase the spread to being worth $20 a share in the scenario of a delay. If the deal closed on time, the $2.62 per share that my option trade cost would end up being worth zero, but we would still make $20 a share on the stock since it would be sold to the LBO buyers for $300 per share.

So my hedging strategy seemed like a win-win. It could cost us $2.62 if the deal closed but would have the potential to turn into as much as $20 a share if it were delayed.

Sounds good, right?

Wrong.

Naively, I didn't take into account what would happen if the deal fell apart completely—if it was not just delayed but squashed. I had devised this complicated option trade that few young traders or risk arbitrageurs were well-versed enough in option modeling to understand, and I was feeling I had done a pretty sophisticated analysis to account for the risk. But I didn't calculate a *completely foreseeable* event—that the deal could fall through.

Let me take you back to the era to give you a sense of the headiness I was feeling. It was the waning years of the '80s—1988 in particular—and the market had fully recovered from the crash of 1987. LBOs were all the rage; it seemed like every day a new, bigger, shinier, flashier LBO was announced, and the size of the deals were growing daily, with banks lending ever-greater amounts. And there I was, right in the heart of things, trading the stocks and options of companies involved in takeover deals. Those companies were the prizes to be won in a crazy carnival of frenzied bidding by LBO firms (also known as private equity firms).

I was not alone in my stupidity. Just as I hadn't foreseen the risk of the deal coming apart, neither did many others who believed the LBO spigot would remain open indefinitely. Teams of bankers searched daily for the next company to target for a buyout. Very few were thinking about whether the companies could withstand the burden of the financial stress (the debt) that these LBOs involved.

A company that needs to use all its cash flow to pay down debt can't very well invest in its stores or in research and development. Fruit of the Loom was a big LBO deal of the late '80s financed by Drexel Burnham Lambert. It's a pretty simple business—they make T-shirts and underwear. However, they had so much debt, and so little margin for error, that the plan to modernize their factories to remain competitive couldn't happen when all the profits went to pay the interest on their debt. Net-net. Like too many other LBO companies of the era, they went bankrupt.

Of course, there was also the very real possibility that the economy could slow down and the earnings these LBO companies were expecting wouldn't materialize either. Yet almost no one was focusing on the downside risk—the seemingly small likelihood that something really bad *could* happen. This is one of the great lessons I've learned about euphoria and panic. People extrapolate way out into the future a continuation of the environment of right now. Yet the market, the economy, and the psyches of investors are cyclical. Things go up and they go down. Things turn around. We can hear it if we listen. *Turn, turn, turn . . . A time to gain, a time to lose.*

As you might have guessed by now, that small chance that the UAL deal would not come to pass became reality. As the deal fell apart, I remember sitting at my computer screen. The market had closed. I saw a headline crossing the tape. I'm paraphrasing, but the gist was: "Talks Fall Apart, UAL CEO Returns from Japan with No Financing." My heart sank, my stomach seized. If the deal had closed, we expected to make about $400,000 (a lot of money in 1989). But in the end, we lost many, many multiples of that expected $400,000. Millions and millions of dollars (that was also a lot of money in 1989). The "brilliant" option trade I had devised that had cost us $2.62 to put on actually cost us an additional *$80* to get out of by the time the dust settled. So the math wasn't put up $2.62 to make $20 or to lose the $2.62. It was put up the $2.62 to make $20, but take on uncertain risk of a magnitude beyond your worst nightmare. Doesn't seem so "brilliant" when you put it that way. It was an outcome that I had not made any provision for. It was devastating. We lost more than I could have imagined.

Besides the money we lost on my "brilliant" hedge, we also lost a fortune on the stock we owned that I was attempting to "hedge." The collapse of the UAL deal, in fact, was the shock wave that literally put an end to the roaring LBO deals of the '80s until they gradually returned a half decade later.

That unrecognized asymmetric risk was the worst trade of my career (as of the present day—and I hope it remains so for the rest of my career). The likelihood that the deal could fall through seemed so small that I didn't even consider it. But the magnitude of the potential loss was breathtaking—or more precisely, nauseating. (By the way, remember that options class all about risk and reward that I loved? Well, that revered Fin 6 professor took the risk of manipulating the price of securities held by an investment company he managed to make the firm look as if their assets were worth more than they actually were. The teacher wound up in prison, and I believe the company went under anyway. How's that for asymmetric risk?)

Before we look at how these risks show up in all areas of our lives, I want to tell you one other investment story. The UAL story was about an asymmetric risk where the downside (unrecognized) far outweighed the upside. But this is the story of the opposite. It's what all of us want, though it's rare. It's the home run.

Wait for the Big Fat Pitch Right over the Plate and Swing

Forever changed by the UAL experience, at Metropolitan we looked to find an asymmetric risk where we could *make*—not lose—multiples on our money. Seems straightforward enough. The search uncovered a hidden gem.

Every once in a while, the investment stars align and serve up the perfect opportunity. It's usually something that not everyone is looking at, and it may actually not be so compelling from the outside, until you look deeper. The truly great opportunities give you more than one way to win. We found just such an opportunity in 2009 in a company called Golar.

We believed (and still believe) that the world's energy needs will continue to grow. We also believed that natural gas would be increasingly viable and valuable as a fuel alternative for countries around the world who wanted to diversify from oil (for political, economic, and environmental reasons) but who didn't have the internal natural resources to meet their demand. In particular, we believed demand for natural gas would grow in Japan and China, which don't have their own supplies. So far, that's all very straightforward.

We wanted to bet on the rising demand for natural gas in Asia, and we wanted to do it in the purest way possible. We didn't want to bet on new natural gas development projects that take years to build and seem to always have "unexpected" delays and obstacles. Nor did we want to bet on the price of natural gas in the United States because it's a very different market than the price in Asia due to supply/demand dynamics and the enormous transportation costs. However, we did want to bet that the amount of liquid natural gas (LNG) to be transported around the world would rise. And we knew the number of ships available and capable of that transportation would grow only slowly due to the time to build those ships, the capital necessary, and the unique expertise required.

We kept our eyes on one of our favorite investors, John Fredriksen from Norway, as he sought to invest in that same theory. Fredriksen is a modern-day Horatio Alger who rose from humble beginnings as the son of a welder. He began his career in a shipbroking company, which is a company that arranges for ships to transport cargoes. The story goes that his fortune was made when he was one of few who continued to transport oil during the Iran-Iraq wars of the 1980s when others thought it was too risky to do so. That risk allowed for gigantic profits, and eventually he became Norway's richest man. He is the anti-Trump in that he likes to maintain a low profile and prefers to keep his name out of the press. We view him as a champion for shareholders. Fredriksen and entities he owned were Golar's biggest shareholder and effectively controlled the company.

Following Fredriksen's lead, we jumped in with a major investment in Golar. In fact, so compelling did we find this opportunity that after we bought as much as we could for our funds (which have self-imposed position size limits), we opened a special purpose fund for investors whose sole holding would be Golar.

Golar was uniquely positioned to be the perfect investment opportunity. It was a pioneer in this relatively new business of transporting LNG. In its gaseous state, this fuel is very voluminous. In order to transport it, it must be cooled to -163 degrees so that it becomes a liquid. That liquid is then transported in unique, highly engineered ships to its desired location where it is then reheated and becomes gaseous once again. Golar was the first company to figure out how to do this process on tankers called FSRUs (floating, storage, and re-gasification units), and no one else in the world had them.

Tankers earn revenue from the party that pays to have a cargo transported. They charge a daily rate for that transportation, not surprisingly referred to as a day rate. The cost to operate a tanker doesn't really change all that much—there are the crew and fuel to operate the ship and some general corporate overhead expenses. Here is the beauty of the tanker business when it works: Day rates can move a lot when there is great demand for large quantities of cargoes to be transported, but the costs of operating those tankers really don't fluctuate a whole lot. As the demand for LNG grew around the world (particularly in Asia), day rates started to spike upward from a depressed low in 2008–09 of about $22,000 per day to an ultimate high well north of $150,000 per day. This increase in rates improves profitability exponentially.

Thus, with our asymmetric Golar investment, several things worked in our favor: (1) Earnings were skyrocketing; (2) the extra cash flow allowed Golar to build more ships to plan to earn even more; and (3) the market started to take notice of this opportunity and bidders flocked to the stock. The shares of Golar, which traded down to $3 a share at the depths of the 2008–09 financial crisis, skyrocketed to the teens and then the twenties—all while the company was paying substantial dividends to shareholders. Then, something extraordinary and completely unexpected happened. The triple earthquake–tsunami–nuclear power catastrophe in Japan on March 11, 2011, caused the trade to go hyperbolic.

As a result of the nuclear meltdown, Japan shut down its nuclear energy capacity. However, the country still needed fuel and switched to natural gas as the most viable alternative. The demand for ships to transport that fuel skyrocketed, and day rates went to over $200,000 per day—nearly 10 times the lows. The stock peaked at over $40 a share (up more than 1,300 percent from its low), which didn't include the dividends that we had received from this investment. This was one of the finest examples of asymmetric risk we had ever seen. While it certainly is not our intent to profit from a tragedy, it does show how unforeseen events can have unexpected consequences, sometimes in your favor, but often not.

Asymmetrical Opportunities

In your life and career, you, too, are going to have the opportunity to get into asymmetrical trades and decisions.

Here's how to evaluate them:

- **Be open to all scenarios in order to create a positive asymmetric risk.** I am always intrigued by the idea of taking on a terrible assignment or challenge—for example, if you are given the opportunity to take over a floundering, money-losing store or division that could be an excellent asymmetric risk. Then, the first thing you should do when you get there is lower your boss's or management's expectations. Many times we see new CEOs brought in to turn around companies and shortly after they take on the job, they announce what is called a "kitchen sink" quarter. That means they reset expectations lower by highlighting all the issues that need to be fixed, throwing everything in—even the "kitchen sink."

By lowering expectations, you've created an opportunity for beating those expectations and made a positive risk/reward profile—that is, a positive asymmetric risk. The upside is if you turn things around, you're a hero. The downside is you're unable to turn around a money-losing business, which isn't the end of the world. Don't rule out the upside and ask yourself, "What could possibly go right?"

- **Look for and assess the unseen.** Always perform your due diligence. I look for blind spots every time I make an investment. Asymmetrical opportunities may be handed to you, or you may make them by yourself. With your eyes wide open, you need to assess the likelihood of the losses *and* the magnitude of the downside if that occurred. If you buy real estate, make deals, or negotiate for a new job, you need to remember, every time, that at least as much thought needs to go into identifying the risks *you don't see* as goes into weighing the risks you do see and making a choice. Some of the unforeseen risks that I learned to look out for the hard way include: the introduction of new regulations that hinder your business; a brand new competitor or powerful existing competitor coming into your own backyard; the loss of the single most important customer you have.

- **Accept the mind-set that the impossible can happen and that we take risks every day.** If I had just realized in the UAL scenario that a complete collapse of the deal was a possibility, albeit small, then I like to think I would have recognized what an unwise risk my option trade was. Now, the wiser me always factors in some likelihood that the impossible can happen. As a portfolio manager, you protect against that by never having all your eggs in one basket. You just cannot know when the highly improbable will become the reality.

Opportunity Knocks

In 1992, while still at DLJ, I realized my career trajectory wasn't going that well. I thought I was doing a decent job, but the environment was so bad on Wall Street at the time and our department had such a narrow mandate ("trade stocks involved in takeover deals," but there weren't any takeover deals getting done in the wake of the LBO collapse). I couldn't see how we were going to be successful.

Yet other parts of Wall Street were starting to perk up. The United States was coming out of the savings and loan (S&L) crisis, and any bank that survived that trauma was poised to make money. There were also lots of bankruptcies and restructurings to focus on from all the broken LBOs that came with the collapse of the roaring '80s. It occurred to me that no matter how smart or clever our team in the arbitrage unit was, we weren't going to do nearly as well as all the people—talented or not—in the restructuring unit simply because there were almost no good risk arbitrage opportunities. It was time to move.

At about the same time I came to that conclusion, Jeffrey Schwarz, my boss from my very first Wall Street job (who became, in turn, a mentor, partner, and lifelong friend), suggested we start a hedge fund. It was a pretty outlandish idea, but he came to me because we liked each other and because I knew a part of the business that Jeffrey knew he wanted to focus on, which was the area of small thrifts. We had begun to focus on it a little bit at the Belzbergs', but it didn't fit into the strategy there. Post–S&L crisis, though, the area was a gold mine. Banks were cheap, and if you knew which ones (i.e., those with very few problem loans and plenty of reserves against any bad ones) to buy, you could do well. It didn't hurt that I was young, ambitious, and seriously hard-working. Plus, without his having to ask, he knew I was available since there was no way I could be feeling optimistic where I was, confined to a mandate with no apparent upside.

He was basically presenting me with an opportunity for great financial upside in exchange for a lot of hard work. The risk was leaving the "big leagues" and cache of a brand-name firm for the scrappy, untested new world of hedge funds—and a start-up to boot. Another negative was going to a much smaller office with a tiny staff and no built-in colleagues to socialize with versus the complete lack of career upside that I then had.

The decision wasn't hard, especially considering that I had no mortgage, no kids, no debt, and no other prospects. Jeffrey even agreed to pay me a guarantee of $25,000 a year so I could eat. This was a gigantic pay cut from where I was, but the upside was so great that the conclusion was easy.

It worked. Fast-forward to today, in which we have made more money than my wildest upside scenarios ever contemplated. I have never regretted that decision. Asymmetric risks aren't always so easy to measure, but we are taking them all the time. Some make sense to take; others defy all logic. Do you ever jaywalk or cross the street against the light? As a typical New Yorker, I do it all the time. Pretty dumb for a mother or four, no? The upside: get across the street faster. The downside: four motherless children and an abandoned husband. I never said I was brilliant.

Asking the Questions: How to Spot Risks Worth Taking

Let me throw out a few questions for you to ponder relating to some asymmetrical risks that you may be overtly or inadvertently signing up for:

Starting Your Own Business

This is a very common and difficult asymmetric risk that many people confront. If it's really your dream and you'll regret not doing it on your deathbed, then clearly you need to factor that in. But for many people, it's a default, like going to law school. (Lawyers out there, don't kid yourself—you know what I mean.) When you weigh the risks of this decision, spend a lot of time defining what your downside is clearly. This way, you will make the best decision possible. For example, define *exactly* how much money you will commit to this endeavor and *exactly* how much time. You can't leave both of those factors open-ended or you're not really defining the risks accurately.

If you don't do that, you are creating a flawed decision-making process, which can lead to a flawed decision and a bad outcome. Of course, you need to weigh factors like where you are in your life, whether you have kids, whether you have a mortgage, and what opportunities or job offers you are forgoing by starting your own business. When you think about starting your own business, begin with the downside as you build the risk/reward model. Don't forget to include feeling responsible for others' livelihoods, constant pressure and responsibility, and that no one will care about its well-being more than you. Employees may view you with a suspect eye. You may very well lose a lot of your own money. A few positives to keep in mind, however, are these: (a) the upside if it works; (b) providing a livelihood for employees; (c) needing less capital than in the past to bring some ideas into being.

For my partner and me, when we started our business, we didn't give it too much thought, or stress that much. He had enough money that he could take the risk. I had just little enough that my downside wasn't all that different from starting and failing to where I was right then. I felt that even if we weren't successful, I had built a resume that included a big-league firm, and Wall Street was improving; therefore, I would be able to get another job. We set a time horizon: We'd try it for a year and a half and see. The hedge fund business was really in its infancy then, and opportunities in this corner of finance were bountiful. It doesn't seem like the environment today provides you with the same chances of success. The hedge fund business has changed dramatically, and it is now decidedly middle-aged. A trifecta has changed the risk/reward scenario dramatically: (1) The space is crowded with a generation of the best and the brightest; (2) the market environment is uncooperative (i.e., more difficult, as we are now a global market, so risks from around the globe must be added to the equation); and (3) the investor base is impatient. But I wouldn't advise anyone against it for those reasons alone. You can't spend your life waiting for the exact right time.

I remember reading a Dear Abby many, many years ago in which a man wrote in saying he wanted more than anything to be a veterinarian, but between the seven years of school and internship, he would be 40 years old when he could finally be a vet. In response, she asked him how old he would be in seven years if he didn't do it.

The Ultimatum

Let me give you another example of a risk I took—this time in my personal life. It's not for the fainthearted. Two and a half years into dating my now husband, I became increasingly aware of and angry about the fact that I knew I wanted to marry him and build a life with him yet he seemed in no hurry whatsoever to get engaged. It was starting to become an issue in the relationship. I had fallen for Lawrence from the moment

I met him. We had an electric chemistry of attraction—not just physical but intellectual as well. I made him laugh, and he cleverly challenged me. And the coolest thing about him is how uncool he is. He doesn't care how he looks, whether most people like him, or if they think he's not cool. He knows who he is. His high school yearbook picture personifies geeky. And yet today, he is undoubtedly handsome. It's almost as if he always knew he would be.

I saw in him a grown-up who wanted to be a family man. I admired the relationship he had with his parents—particularly the respect he had for his mother as a model for his views on women. I had been imagining a life with him for a while, but I was starting to wonder if I was the only one imagining that. We were at a New Year's Eve party in 1992 at a Washington DC town house of an old friend of Lawrence's. Interestingly to me as a Jackie O–phile, the Kennedys' lived in this town home when JFK was a senator and president-elect. I felt no Jackie vibe, however, and was acting the part of a pouty date in a black party dress. The tension between us had been simmering for months. Lawrence was living in Washington as a White House Fellow (a highly prestigious, pretty much do-nothing-but-meet-people one-year internship). I would visit on weekends.

He had asked me to move in with him, but we were not engaged and Jeffrey and I were starting Metropolitan Capital. It didn't seem right to give up my career path to be Lawrence's sidekick and hope we'd become engaged. I had been subtle about my hopes, but increasingly I became angry, and I finally realized that was only making things worse. I'd be heartbroken without him. But this in-between time of not knowing where the relationship was going was heartbreaking as well. So in short, I gave him an ultimatum—a very clear and simple one: Either we're engaged in 60 days or we're done; it was getting too hard. I might have sugarcoated it a little, but that was really the gist of it.

"So you're telling me," Lawrence asked incredulously, "if we're not engaged in 60 days, we're done?"

I replied without hesitation. "Yes, that's the way it works."

And yet, I didn't really think I was taking that big of a risk because either he proposed and we were together (the reward) or he was unable to, in which case I needed to know that. I loved him but I wouldn't wait around forever (the risk of loss). I didn't think the ultimatum would push him away; I really just thought he was stuck. Of course, I still worried.

I remember having dreams of him desperately wanting to marry me so much that he couldn't wait to propose. Well, that didn't happen. In real life as opposed to my dreams, Lawrence is a lot of things, but hopeless romantic isn't one of them. As he says, it's not a la carte.

As I waited and my anxiety mounted, I suggested we go to a marriage counselor to discuss it, which he graciously agreed to do. At our first appointment, the therapist basically asked, "Why are you here?" so I started telling her about the ultimatum.

She then replied, "Are you saying that if you get married, any time in your life if he can't reach a decision, you're going to give him an ultimatum?"

"Well," I considered for just a second, "if he has had sufficient time and information to make a decision and is still unable to do so, then yes, I am," to which my now husband remarked, "That's good enough for me; let's go." He is nothing if not practical.

Shortly thereafter we got engaged. It was my birthday, a winter Thursday in New York City, and we went out for breakfast to Michael's. My birthday is the one day of the year I eat sweets—literally, the only one. I ordered chocolate-chip pancakes. It didn't matter how nervous I was, I was going to eat every last bite. I thought something was up when he had arranged for a limousine to take us to the restaurant. It was the last day we were going to be in the same city before the ultimatum expired—day 58 of 60.

After a few minutes of chatting, Lawrence said, "I'm nervous because I'm going to ask you to marry me," and he presented me with a ring. I hated the ring, though I kept my mouth shut. He laughed as he looked at my expression and said, "Don't worry; it's fake. I bought it from a catalogue. Get whatever you want." As much as he says he's not romantic, that's romance to a Jewish girl.

Lawrence would say that I had to force him; otherwise, he never would have made a decision. This is a guy who won't use his blinkers when he's driving because he doesn't want to give up any options.

Starting a Family

There is no right, ideal, convenient time to try to have a baby (or for many other things that make life and work rewarding). The risk is there—to your health, the baby's health, your career, and your relationship with your husband. There are complications, prematurity, and a whole new way of life that can't be planned for, managed, or controlled.

Babies are joyous, blessed gifts; pregnancies and childcare are, after every superlative is uttered, disruptive. The only thing we can be sure of is that things won't go according to plan and that nothing is exactly as it appears.

Many women I know run through various scenarios about the ideal time to get pregnant, such as, "I want to make vice president before I have kids," or "I don't want to be nine months pregnant in August because I'll be so uncomfortable," or even, "I hate summer maternity clothes, so if I'm due in the spring, I could skip that season altogether."

By trying to wait until the perfect time, you may end up realizing you can't get pregnant. Before you hold off on getting pregnant, consider the risk in waiting. Picture a doctor telling you that you won't be able to have kids naturally and weigh your reaction against your reason for holding off. The flip side of that analysis for many women is whether the risk of having a child during their late 20s and early 30s may derail their chances of moving from an associate to a management level. To this day, I still wonder if I had started earlier if I would have been able to get pregnant without the fertility clinic. Infertility is stressful, an emotional roller coaster, unpredictable in the outcome, and, of course, oh-so-difficult to fit into your schedule.

In my case, the stress of my career was having an impact. This is embarrassing but true. In a moment of frustration paired with intellectual curiosity, Lawrence overlaid my monthly ovulation chart with the stock market, and we were shocked to discover that the up-and-down cycle of the market matched the up-and-down notations of my ovulation cycles. How's that for unknowable risk?

The takeaway here is that we're taking risks all the time whether or not we choose to see it. Risk is not in itself a bad thing. Women shouldn't shy away from risks; we just need to make good, calculated bets. We need to be sure that when we take risks, we do so with our eyes wide open. Not considering the upside or downside of a situation doesn't prevent it from happening. We can't wait around forever until everything feels riskless and safe—it doesn't work that way. No risk, no reward. Simple.

CHAPTER 5

Find Your Inner Decider

In my house, I'm the boss, my wife is just the decider.
—Woody Allen

It is no accident that emotions are one of the flavors of risk that financial planners advise their clients about. There's market risk (stocks go up, stocks go down), interest rate risk (your bond investments can't keep pace with inflation), and emotional risk (you sell in a panic and buy at a peak). As an investor, I've learned that I can't control the stock market. But I can control my emotions, so why not remove that risky variable from my decision making?

This isn't the only area of decision making where I need improvement. There are several, and the better I get at each one, the better my life becomes. The first and maybe toughest decision-making change for women is learning the difference between deciding and polling.

Deciding versus Polling

All of us need to make decisions every day—some big, some small, and most, inconsequential. For women especially, learning how to make better decisions more confidently can change everything:

> *Better process = Better decisions*
> *Better decisions = Better outcomes*

We don't need to reinvent the wheel every time we face a major decision. We need a road map, if you will, to point the way.

Have you ever found yourself in this situation: You're in a shoe store trying to decide which black pumps to buy and you're soliciting advice from other customers in the store whom you don't even know?

Then, you may feel obliged to take their opinion into account when you make a decision even if you have no basis on which to judge whether you may value their opinion? Also notice that the person you ask will almost always push you to get them with some compliment about how great you and/or the shoes look. Have you ever done that same thing? We like the good feeling of complimenting other women in order to make them feel good—it makes us feel good. Imagine a man walking out of a dressing room and approaching two men that he doesn't know and asking, "Could these pants go from the office to a party?"

I've tried to learn something from men about decisiveness in the department store. It really is liberating. I remember not too long ago going to Saks to buy a pair of black pumps for work along with a pair of evening shoes for an event. I tried on three or four pairs and then said, "I'll take these and those."

The salesman, rather surprised, said, "That's it? You've decided?"

Just that easily, I'd decided. I just wasn't going to give that decision too much room in my mind. Would it necessarily change the outcome to go over every detail of each shoe in a compare/contrast exercise? In the end, would it really matter? It helps to also realize that the future of the planet doesn't rest on every decision.

Data Collecting Is Not Deciding

Too many women think they are deciding when they are polling. It's similar to leading by consensus building, which I am not a fan of either. When you poll everyone, a few dynamics are at work: You may want to include everyone's thoughts, to get "the village" to answer. You may feel like the burden of the decision will rest less squarely on your shoulders alone.

By amassing all this "polling data," you may hope that one of the respondents will have that magical answer, the one that makes it so perfectly clear what the right thing to do is.

This isn't going to happen. You may think for a moment after you hear something that it was the magical answer, but then later over drinks that evening or in a late-night conversation with your best friend or significant other, you may get an opposing magical answer. Stop hoping decision making involving a complex issue will be easy—it isn't. And if it's not a complex issue, then why bother with all the polling? Some opinions of those polled don't really matter to you anyway. And it just pisses people off when you always ask for their advice and never follow it.

Make the decision and own it. And if you're not yet the official authority, own your recommendation. If it's within the scope of your role, consider making more decisions; you'll see a learning curve in the process.

Consciously develop an approach that works for you and that you can repeat. It will get you through some really tough moments. It will give you confidence. It will push you to be more decisive with more ease than you imagined.

And remember, the bigger the stakes, the more important the decision-making process. The quality and effectiveness of the choices you make are going to be affected by it. In fact, I truly believe that just the process itself can help.

Six Steps toward Better Decision Making

What follows is my map—the habits, or rules, that help me describe a problem and dissect it calmly:

1. Frame the problem.
2. Understand your emotions and take them out of the equation.
3. Know your options; ask the questions.
4. Look for the 51 percent solution—surrender to the gray.
5. Recognize what needs to be decided now and what doesn't.
6. Cut your losses.

Of course, you don't need to follow *my* regimen, but you must develop *a* regimen.

1. Frame the Problem

You have to clearly define the problem. Get rid of the extraneous noise that clouds the problem and clouds your judgment. This noise is usually your feelings, worries, expectations, and fears, not the problem itself.

You need to recognize when you're emotional. More precisely, you need to clarify what those emotions are and how they can confuse the issue you're working through. The emotions keep you from seeing what the real goal is. To frame the problem, you need to have the end goal in mind. Are you trying to score an apology or is there a larger or different goal in sight?

Here's a familiar scenario: You and your significant other are on your way to your best friend's party. However, you're late because your Better Half (husband, boyfriend, partner) didn't really think you needed to get there at a certain time or didn't care or had other things to get done before you left. You get angry and indignant on the ride over, thinking you'll explain what he did wrong and get your frustration out of your system, and he'll repent and ask for forgiveness. Does it ever go like that? No. (Note to reader: If this isn't your typical scenario, pick another one.)

The habit of confronting and fighting doesn't take into consideration the real goal and thus the real problem.

The situation is you're late and you're pissed. The natural response would be to have a fight in the car, but does staging *Who's Afraid of Virginia Woolf* in an SUV get you any closer to your goal of having a good time at the party?

A fight does not. But maybe if you did the counterintuitive thing and dismantled your anger, there could be an extra benefit: good will and affection between your significant other and your best friend. There's little chance of that if you walk in the door of your friend's party fresh from a shouting match.

I also have come to the conclusion that sometimes Lawrence is hoping for the fight (and I'm sure the shoe is on the other foot often enough, too). Rather than my securing the hoped-for apology, he's maybe angling for an escalation of the argument into something that ends with his not going.

A moment of reflection recalibrates the situation. If the goal is to have a good time, it's much easier to set aside the stress of leaving, feeling late, wondering if he wanted to go, and calming the waters. This might look like I'm allowing him to be passive aggressive, but I also recognize I may be overreaching, so I try to keep the big picture in mind. Here's one of my personal mantras on marriage or raising your kids: "Pick your spots"—everything can't be a hot button, so I need to focus on the ones I simply cannot ignore.

At the office, staying clear about the big goals can get rid of hours of discussion, blaming, information gathering, and expense. I came to a realization that I spent a lot of time feeling beleaguered and irritated by little tasks that I had to do at work. I was constantly bombarded by requests for approvals for bills or wire instructions, or my sign-off on minutely small decisions regarding our trading strategies, such as which broker to use to execute a trade. The end goal for me was to be able to focus on the big-picture parts of the business. I knew I had smart people around me, yet they seemed in need of constant hand-holding.

But I had it wrong. I had created this system perhaps out of a misguided desire to be in control or needed. I had never empowered them to make decisions on things that they were perfectly capable of handling. It occurred to me that this level of oversight was not so fun for them and it probably gave them a sense that I didn't trust them, when in fact, I did. Decision made. I knew I had to delegate. It was better for me and for them.

I made a list of what was taking up my time and energy and what I needed to keep doing and what I really could let go. I can't and don't want to delegate wire instructions. I need to see every significant amount of money that flows out of the firm—every single one—but for many other things I could easily be out of the loop. Rather than cause a bottleneck, I could just get out of the way and focus on making more consequential decisions.

I learned this:

If decisions are not of great consequence, don't give them a lot of space.

- What is the deadline or amount of time you'll allot to work on the solution? A lot of stress and confusion can be relieved by getting to a solution faster if it's not a critical decision (just decide on the window treatment, or logo, or office procedure already, and remove the burden and pressure).
- What is the bottom-line outcome that needs to happen? Can it change or is it immovable?

Are you crystal clear about the decision you need to make? Can you say it in one sentence? It's a great exercise to test your focus and the real issue at hand.

2. Understand Your Emotions and Take Them Out of the Equation

Just as no situation is helped by losing your temper, neither are good decisions made when you are emotional. It cannot help. Ever.

Back in mid-2007, Susan Krakower and Mary Duffy, two producers from CNBC, called me about joining the CNBC show *Fast Money*. They'd seen me in a magazine called *Trader Monthly* in an article entitled "Women of Wall Street." At that time, I already felt stretched pretty thin.

Lawrence and I had two sets of twins, Lucy and Jack who were then ten, and Kate and William, then six-year-olds. My husband runs his own investment firm that lends to middle-market buyouts and as such, he works sixty hours a week. He is extremely hands-on and often takes the lead with the kids' schoolwork, planning vacations, and running the house, which leaves him pretty stretched, too. I put the kids to bed every night, pay the bills, take the kids shopping for clothes, and make the play dates but never cook. Our housekeeper helps usher them out the door in the mornings when I'm usually working out. I try to be home every night before bedtime—about 80 to 90 percent of the time I accomplish that.

The younger twins still want us to lie down with them for a few minutes, so we do, and I love those quiet moments of chatting. Even if we've been together a few hours before bedtime, those moments are the most precious. It's not my yelling at them to brush and floss, but rather them asking if one of their ideas for an invention could work, telling us what they want to be for Halloween, wondering how many kids they'll have, or whatever. After that bedtime, Lawrence and I check in with the big twins who may or may not need our help. We try to get them to commit to a bedtime. Then, sometimes, we have a few minutes to ourselves, though very few.

Our lives seemed pretty full. There was very little air in either of our days. There was no Me Time, no He Time, and We Time consisted of one dinner alone per week on "date night." And then the *Fast Money* opportunity arrived like the last straw on the camel's back.

Several weeks into the TV show, when I clearly was not able to manage it all, Lawrence said to me, "Something's gotta give." As he said it, I already knew it to be true. The situation had become untenable. I thought I had become a master of multitasking. Instead I was just mucking things up. Exhibit 1: Since I was so stressed and was having such trouble sleeping, I would take an Ambien an hour before bed. Then, in an attempt to be highly efficient, I would dash off some quick emails before bed thinking I'd get a few items out of my in-box and back into someone else's. After an embarrassing email to the CEO of a company we were investors in where I misspelled the word *green* as *grean* and my own name and then proceeded to wipe out all, and I mean *all*, of the data on my BlackBerry (a feat I could not recreate fully awake with a $100,000 incentive), I realized something had to change.

Of course, refraining from EUI (email under the influence) was a no-brainer. A simple fix.

But clearly I had a few decisions to make.

At first, I felt angry at my husband and thought the only problem was that he was not being supportive and understanding enough. I rationalized that what I really needed was just more help at home: If he could just pick up a little more slack, everything would be so much easier and I wouldn't be feeling so overwhelmed.

But in my heart I knew that Lawrence's pointing out the problem wasn't the actual problem. He really does do more than his share. Subliminally, I was just blaming the messenger. I knew I needed to get much clearer about what I really wanted to do and make rational decisions about how I could accomplish that. The sleepless nights were undermining my ability to do this.

The very next weekend, with Lawrence's blessing and willingness to take over my share of the childcare responsibilities, I gave myself one long day to rest and actually work through my own decision-making process. I needed to frame the problem. Originally, I thought my husband was the problem—that's how I *felt*. But of course, he wasn't the problem. He wasn't asking or telling me to make a choice about my priorities. He was telling me that if I wanted to continue to do the show, I needed to run my life more efficiently.

It sounded very cold, and it didn't address my emotional state, but it was the truth. Sometimes I want him to help me in the girl way, which means saying, "Wow, this must be so stressful for you." And sometimes, such as then, I need help in the boy way, with specific advice like "Rearrange your schedule to work out before the kids get up." More sympathy and understanding weren't going to make things better in a practical way.

So on that quiet weekend morning, with my emotions on pause, one thing stood out: I really did want to do the show. When I pictured giving it up and imagining how that would be, I knew I couldn't.

This was a whole new adventure. I was enjoying learning new skills, meeting new people, and getting introduced to a whole new business. Plus, it was fun. It's remarkable how people look at you differently when you are on TV—even cable TV. The people I already knew were markedly friendlier, and some people that I only knew of, now seemed to know me, which is fun (Carl Icahn, for example). So the problem changed from *What do I have to give up?* into *How do I structure my life to allow me to do what I wanted to do?*

It was necessary for me to take the emotion out of the equation so that I could get to the essence of the problem. It wasn't about being angry at my husband, and it wasn't about having to give up some of the things I loved to do, like looking at modern art or talking to my girlfriend Donna on the phone late, late at night or watching the occasional low-brow TV show that I can't admit to. I was quite willing to do that. It was about solving the puzzle of making room for this new experience.

I should have recognized right away that emotions and fatigue had gotten the better of me. The current structure was overwhelming, but it didn't have to be as bad as I was making it, wearing my overwork and exhaustion like badges of honor. I don't know what I was trying to prove or to whom.

Oddly, I knew that emotions could control my day job as an investor / hedge fund manager. I spent years recognizing when emotions were getting in the way, yet I couldn't see it clearly in this new endeavor.

If you have been led to believe that emotions are the truth, the heart of authenticity and intuition that will set you free, you need to let that go. Trust your gut, sure. But know that emotions can be toxic when it comes to decision making.

This is a particular problem for women.

Consider this:

- What is your gut reaction telling you (it's there, so acknowledge it)?
- Can you firmly answer yes or no to the decision? If you produce a firm answer, you can figure out the solutions.
- Can you identify specific emotions that are getting in the way of your decision making, such as blame, guilt, pride, fear, or anxiety?
- How can you lower the emotional stakes to allow for more clear thinking?
- What nonemotional, practical options are there for solving the problem or making the decision?
- Can you get help for the emotional part of the equation (from a friend, trusted advisor, therapist)?

3. Know Your Options; Ask the Questions

Once you've framed the problem and gotten a grip on your emotions, you need to identify the actual options available to you. Remember, what we're trying to do is bigger than making a good choice this one time. We're trying to build a model that will help us make better decisions every time. We're making a manual.

For me to continue to be on CNBC and do my day job, I had to understand my options to make it work better since I had decided I wanted to try to do both. So I asked myself how I could use my time better and more efficiently. What was taking so much of my time? Were there any tasks I could skip?

One habit that I've learned as an investor that is now second nature to me in my personal life is to force myself to think one step ahead. It's as easy as just asking, "What might happen next?"

If you're negotiating a deal, you might ask, What will happen if we say no? What options will they come back with? What will happen if we lose the deal?

One thing I didn't realize with the TV show but that I ask myself now when things come up is this: Will I get used to the issue that is feeling so problematic? Will some parts of it get easier if I just do them enough times?

It didn't occur to me then that I would get more comfortable in front of the camera and that eventually I would feel confident enough to know I would not have to prepare every single thing I was going to say—I could just have a few bullet points.

On a practical level, I needed to be more efficient about two major drags on my time—getting made-up and buying clothes for the show. I realize that sounds petty, but when I broke down the problem to what was really taking my time and causing stress in my schedule, hair, makeup, and clothes were the culprits. I needed to figure out a way to buy many outfits at once and set up relationships at stores where people knew my sizes and likes and could just call me when they saw something just right for me (and the camera). Or if I found something that worked, I could get it in a few different colors.

I also negotiated with the network that they would come to my office every day to do hair and makeup. This was actually key to making it all work. I could still exercise in the morning and put my hair in a wet ponytail after showering.

I could still be at my desk while they made me look camera-ready, and I wouldn't have to leave my office until after the market closed. That last point was an absolute deal breaker. It was preventing me from doing my day job in the way I needed to.

I had to keep asking myself, How can I do it better, faster, easier? For some things, there is *not* an easier way. But it turns out that for hair and makeup, there is. I was starting to find my sea legs. I just might be able to make this work. For my triathlete sister, Stacey, she simplifies the time choosing work outfits daily by laying them all out for the week on Sunday. To her that's enough time saved each day to run an extra mile.

Defining your options as clearly as possible is a step we can't skip. We need to ask the questions about our options but without emotion and while we keep the end goal in sight. CNBC was a work decision; let me show you how I've used the same process to keep all the balls in the air that I need to as a working mother of four children.

At home with my kids, the goal is this: I want them to know that they are loved and that I care about them. Sometimes conflicts obscure the goal. For the annual art show where the second graders display their art projects for the year, Kate and William, aged six at the time, were crushed when I told them I had a conflict.

Kate is effervescent. She literally skips through her day and nothing gets her down. She's the optimist who is excited about everything and conscientious, and if it says "parents can attend," she will make sure one of us is duly there.

William, on the other hand, holds his emotions much closer to the vest and occasionally lets a small smile spread across his face. I know he wants me to see his artwork, but he's quite masterful at pretending he doesn't really care.

After going through the logistics of getting home after *Fast Money* to drive up to school together (we live in Manhattan, and our four children attend a private school in the Riverdale section of the Bronx), I realized we'd never make it in time. With traffic, we could arrive well beyond late, and I imagined the frustration and simmering stress we'd all feel on the car ride. I came up with an alternate plan: The nanny could take them to school, and I could meet them there for the second half of the art show. I added the treat of staying out extra late (for a school night) to get ice cream afterward. Everyone was happy with that. Always, the question is, Am I accomplishing my goal and making sure they feel and know I care about them? Whatever your specific situation, just ask the questions.

Ask yourself this:

- What am I trying to accomplish, and how will I know I have done it?
- To whom does it matter?
- How big are the stakes, and for whom?
- What specific options are there? What else is available as an option? Does a colleague, a child, a spouse have any ideas? Sometimes you do need to get out of your own head to discover lots of choices.
- How much does it cost, and how complicated is it?
- Can I do it with the knowledge and resources I have?
- What will happen next—what do I learn if I think one step ahead?

- Will I get better at it? Will time help? Will I get used to it?

4. Look for the 51 Percent Solution—Surrender to the Gray

This isn't a joke about hair color. In fact, I'll probably go to my grave still insisting I'm a true blond, which I truly was till my teens. It's about starting your decision process from the fact that the world is not the black and white we knew it to be as children. Issues are complicated. Allegiances can pull you in multiple directions. You need to accept that in many aspects of your career and personal life, the issues and choices will be gray.

We need to have realistic expectations about the outcome of our decisions. Many of the questions we face are complex, and each side of the decision may have many points in its favor. That's why decision making can be very hard, obviously. *From murky equations and trade-offs, we cannot expect to have a crystal clear answer.*

What I propose is this:

Accept the murkiness and aim for the 51 percent solution.

That is, find the right answer that you can feel good about at least 51 percent of the time. You cannot hope that each decision leads to an outcome where you are delighted all the time. Otherwise, decision making wouldn't be the least bit challenging.

For many women, certainly not all, one of the most complex, difficult, controversial, emotional, entangled decisions we face is whether to stay home with the children or go back to work. This one decision polarizes factions of women and polarizes feelings within many women. I'm not seeking here to campaign for either side. It's a personal decision. For me, though, it was easy; I was going back to work, without a doubt. That was the right answer.

For women who are torn, please recognize that the perfect decision isn't out there. There is only the compromise that leaves you feeling as if you made the right choice most of the time—even if it's only a tiny bit past split evenly. *Occasional feelings of ambivalence are a by-product of the process of making a difficult decision, not evidence of a mistake.* Think one step ahead and anticipate these feelings so you won't be thrown off course when they emerge, which they invariably will.

If you're the stay-at-home mom who feels pangs of regret when you hear about exciting things ex-colleagues are doing, or if you're the executive who has to go on a business trip and miss Back-to-School Night *again* and you're feeling as if you've let your kids down and are a poor excuse for a mother, remember—this ambivalence is to be expected. It's not the sign of having made a wrong decision.

In fact, there is no way to ensure you're being a "good" mother anyway. I had a baby shower for my friend Janet. The theme of the shower was that each person needed to tell Janet a piece of advice about parenting, if relevant, or a story about the worst thing your parents had done to you as a child. It sounds horrible. It was hilarious. But there was a gem here for any working mother.

The one story that stuck with me now for a decade was from Janet's friend Miranda, who told the story of how she came to be a guest panelist on the *Oprah Winfrey Show* to talk about what it was like to grow up with a mother who worked (in the '60s and early '70s, when most moms didn't). Miranda did the taping, all went well, and when she found out when it would air, she excitedly told her mom the news that she was going to be on the show and made a date so they could watch it together. Well, the show opened with Oprah making a big fuss about the pioneering women who worked when their kids were still small and at home and how those pioneer kids coped, and what moving stories they were going to share. Her mom gasped.

"What do you mean your mom worked?" her shocked mother blurted out. "I quit my job for seven years to stay home with you." Miranda hadn't remembered it that way.

As a working mom, I found this story hilarious. If you're a stay-at-home mom, it's probably not so funny. So much for how we remember things and how we think our kids will remember them. We can try our best to be perfect, yet our children will grow up remembering some shortcoming we didn't even see.

Use these tools to work through to a 51 percent decision:

- Write an actual pro and con list and then ask yourself out loud, and answer out loud, how you would feel if you said yes, or no, to the decision.
- Literally ask yourself if you can live with the decision. Go back to your options and ask the questions to get more clarity and more choices to make one solution work better—just 1 percent better.
- Act "as if" you made one choice for one week (or one day, depending on the time frame) and see how the de-

cision fits. Do the reverse. You don't need to share the decision. You need to *own it* for that period of time and act *as if*.

5. Recognize What Needs to Be Decided Now and What Doesn't

I try to learn something of value anywhere I can. In 1999, I was attending our littlest sister Stacey's graduation from Wharton. Robert Rubin, former head of Goldman Sachs and secretary of the treasury under President Clinton, was the speaker. I honestly love a good commencement address. I can usually learn something, whether it's a great quote, a really funny saying, or a lesson that will stick with me. If I just come away with one single thing, I will feel enriched.

That day, Bob Rubin was talking about his career. To be honest, this wasn't setting up to be the best day. Most non–Wall Streeters were probably disappointed in the choice of speakers. It was searingly hot and humid and, well, we were in Philadelphia. And just to add one more element of delight to the oppressive heat, my entire family was there, a recipe for irritation if not disaster. There is nothing quite like thousands of family members sitting on hot metal bleachers at Franklin Field (a monument to the mediocrity of Ivy League football) in search of that one black diamond cap that you came to see.

Yet for me on that spring day in 1999, I could relax. Our portfolio had rebounded quite nicely after a tumultuous 1998. The economy was humming along, employment was steady, and the biggest threat on the horizon seemed to be Y2K. (Yes, these are the types of things I think about.)

Naturally, I hung on every word of Rubin's story. It was

like sitting at the feet of a master of my financial universe, and it didn't really matter how enlightening, or not, he would be. I was listening for that one gem. And then he said it—something so profound (to me) that I think it was lost on a large part of the audience. What he said was this:

When you have a big decision to make, wait as long as you can before deciding.

Now, that may not seem so earth-shattering, but it woke me up to something. He went on to explain that the reason to delay is that during that period of waiting you may get access to additional information that will give you more clarity in making the decision.

This wasn't procrastination or indecisiveness. It was his conscious approach to preparing, making a plan, and knowing exactly what and when he needed to make a decision. Ah, what simple common sense. The simplest truths resonate so thoroughly. It's as if you've always known them, even if you never realized it before.

Rubin's waiting-as-long-as-you-can approach might be counterintuitive and counter to what your colleagues and bosses might want, yet it gave Rubin a very clear path. He would be fully prepared when a major decision point arrived.

To this day, that speech made me realize that it's OK to say, "Let's have that fight (or debate) when we get to it." Not making a premature decision is a sign of maturity. A judge would say, "The issue is not ripe for adjudication," meaning, we don't need to solve the problem today. Setting something aside for another day, month, or year can be thoughtful and wise.

Trying to get through a laundry list of decisions because you've finally found a bit of time to do so means the last few items on the list will often get short shrift and be decided in such haphazard a way as "Let's split the difference" or "I'm too tired to argue with you." This helps no one, least of all the organization or important relationships. Kicking the can for decisions that *need* to be made is *not* a solution (which is hitting us squarely in the face as a nation) because you often foreclose some options. However, leaving a decision that doesn't need to be made is.

I remember facing the question of whether we needed to hire more staff. The fund was growing, as were the amount of accounting and back-office functions necessary. That part of the decision seemed clear.

The problem was, increasing our staff meant we were going to be too big for our space, which triggered another question: What should we do about our lease and finding new space? This led to other questions about how long a lease we would feel comfortable signing and finally to the big question of how long my partner and I wanted to keep working, as in the practical matter of a 5-year lease or a 10-year lease.

As we worked through the decision trees, we had to weigh each branch. We did need additional support—that was easy to decide. We were prepared to find new space, even though it was an enormous time sink. But there was no way we were prepared or willing to decide how long we wanted to keep the firm going, at least under our leadership.

Knowing that indeterminate detail, we were able to negotiate a medium-term lease with some options for extensions. This may (or may not) have cost us more than a longer-term lease because the market was so hot at the time, but we recognized that we were willing to pay a little more to keep our options open. We would revisit that decision about how long we wanted to keep working on another day.

Ask yourself this:

- Can I decide right now? Is a bias toward sooner good, whenever possible?
- Can I make a tentative decision and hold off on the final assessment until the actual deadline (so new information can come to light, in Bob Rubin's framework)?
- Is there an externally imposed deadline? If not, what is *your* deadline?
- Can you take it off the table—mentally and emotionally?
- What is the opportunity cost of not deciding? In economic terms, an opportunity cost is the opportunity sacrificed when another choice is made. In decision-making terms, it's the cost of not moving on. Does leaving the decision still open weigh on you / your team? Might you lose some of the options open to you now? For example, let's say you meet an interesting candidate to join your firm but are not sure you need the additional firepower right then. Could someone else hire her in the interim? Would you be OK with that?

6. Cut Your Losses

This is perhaps one of the most important lessons I've learned not just in investing, but in life. I've mishandled this lesson countless times, but it is imperative to remember.

There's a saying for investors, "You're first loss is your best loss," which basically means taking a small loss at first may be the very best trade you can make. Let's revisit the United Airlines trade. As the UAL deal broke, the stock cratered from about $280 to $230 a share. This cost us dearly, *but* because we were too slow to react to the reality that the deal had broken, *and* we were relying on hope, we held on to the trade all the way down to $160. That second move was what really cost us.

Sometimes investments don't work out the way you think or hope they will. I find it's helpful to have a clear-cut set of events that would trigger a sale of a position. By setting parameters up before I make an investment, I remove the emotion and ego that may hinder my ability to make good decisions after an investment that I've made starts to go against us and we are losing money. I sell if one of the following things happens: (1) I lose faith in management because they lied to me or misled me; (2) I lose faith in management because it's clear they don't have a handle on their business; (3) new, unexpected regulations threaten the business; (4) the company gets into a new, unrelated line of business from its core competency; (5) I bought the stock for a specific event which has happened—regardless of whether the event turned out the way I was hoping or not—or finally (6) I lose the preset amount I have allotted to be lost in any one trade.

I think about cutting my losses all the time, not just in investing—for example, if I've hired the wrong person and it's clear things will not work out. Or if you're in the wrong relationship (you know it in your heart). I've widened the concept of cutting my losses as I've gotten older. Let's say I buy tickets to the opera and it turns out I really hate it. I give it a chance, but I no longer give in to some sense of duty or the worry that everyone is watching. I leave. Life is too short.

If you've made a very big decision where things were gray and you went for the 51 percent answer but now realize you chose the 49 percent answer, allow yourself to change your mind—but only after you've really given yourself a realistic amount of time to determine the true answer.

The Risk of Avoiding Decisions

What I want to leave you with is that you can learn something from men about being decisive. It doesn't have to be so hard. Though wishing you were more decisive won't make it so, you can use the habits of decision making to become as decisive as you need to be.

Frame the problem. Separate your emotions. Figure out the options—lots of them. Ask the questions. Get comfortable with the gray. Whenever you can, and as a general habit, for the small stuff, decide quickly. For rare and really big stuff—think Bay of Pigs—follow Rubin's advice. Execute your plan, keep your antennae up, and wait till the last possible moment, with the latest information available, to pull the trigger and make your decision official.

Practice and develop better decision-making habits, and stop asking strangers in department stores, "Do these shoes look good on me?"

CHAPTER 6

Fail Well

I've missed more than 9,000 shots in my career. I've lost almost 300 games. Twenty-six times I've been trusted to take the game-winning shot and missed. I've failed over and over and over again in my life. And that is why I succeed.

—Michael Jordan

Several years ago, I was speaking to a group of graduates at my alma mater, the Wharton School at the University of Pennsylvania (I'm not graduation-speech timber yet like Bob Rubin, but I do just fine with a small group). I wanted to give them some real-world advice. I wanted to share those kernels of wisdom that seem so obvious to me now but that I wish someone would have told me when I was sitting in that very same auditorium years before, hoping the speaker would stop talking. (By the way, if you're the speaker, be brief. It is the best advice I can give any presenter in any setting, anywhere.)

I predicted a few of the things they would encounter:

A number of them would be wildly successful, though I didn't know which ones.

A number of them who could never get dates would find themselves to be the belle or prince of the ball, though, who are we kidding? The prince of the ball would likely also be the one who found himself to be wildly successful.

And each of them, every single one, would fail at some point in their lives. Nothing was as important as this thought. Failure is guaranteed. While I hope I had some other witty and helpful things to say, the most important was that failure was, in fact, the only thing they could count on as they headed out into the world.

As I explained, every successful person you meet will cite failure, along with luck and hard work, as instrumental in their development. Yet, and I'm loath to admit it, too many women continue to be afraid to fail. What's more, we often perceive that men aren't. Maybe men are and maybe they aren't, but it doesn't matter. They're much better at trying anyway.

Since you can't avoid failure, the sooner you learn to expect and prepare for it—in both its real and imagined forms—the happier and more successful you'll be.

We—especially women—need to be vigilant about three kinds of failure that can undermine us:

- The fear of failure
- The failure to be proactive
- The failure to execute successfully—that is, really screwing something up—which is the most popular

The Fear of Failure

Fearing failure can be a paralyzing trap that becomes a self-fulfilling prophecy. You've seen one of those posters that says something like this:

YOU MISS 100 PERCENT OF THE SHOTS YOU DON'T TAKE

I know—you're thinking to yourself, "Wow, that's corny." But you get the message on some level, and it gives you a moment of inspiration. We fail if we don't give ourselves the chance to take the shot.

Over and over again, throughout your education, career, and life, you're going to have to make a decision to act, to pursue things that seem out of your reach, to force yourself to get past the fear of failure.

The first step, which is always my personal starting point, is plain and simple: Live with the fear—too bad.

But it really is more complicated than that, since our fears can be insidious lurkers. When you can't simply boss your fears around, here are some of my techniques for getting over your fear of failure.

When I was first contemplating accepting the offer to be on CNBC, I remember being very afraid of what people would say. No "serious" hedge fund manager had ever done such a thing. Part of what made hedge funds so alluring and what glamorized the players was that no one was talking. The more hidden it was, the more intriguing. What would my colleagues in the industry say about me? Well, isn't it ironic to say, "I'm a hedge fund manager; I have a reputation to uphold"? What if the show failed? What if I failed? What would they think?

Intellectually I knew that other people's expectations and opinions of me should never determine my actions. In fact, I am drawn to investments that everyone seems to hate because I think they often set up the best risk/reward propositions. I'm happiest when I'm investing far from the thundering herd. Yet I would be lying if I said that I didn't care what other people thought of me. Joanna Coles from *Cosmo* relates, "It's important to be open to unexpected opportunities, 'taking the call,' and never being afraid to make a move or do the unexpected or take a job others don't approve of."

I talked myself through my real and imagined fears as well as the risks and rewards. If I were to give up this opportunity I valued because of the perceived downside of what someone else *may* say, what would it mean for other opportunities that might come? Would it mean that I had tapped out on the risks I would take and it was now time to play it safe and do what everyone else did? How would I feel if I hesitated too long and they gave the offer to someone else? That seemed like an equal recipe for disaster. Companies—and marriages and friendships—that stagnate, fail. I was ready to say yes and take the shot.

I called and said yes to the offer a week after it had been made, and after a brief negotiation, I reached out to share the news with the few friends and colleagues I'd confided in to gauge their response. Well, here's the truth: They weren't really thinking about it all that much, except maybe for a passing second. A few thought it was great, one was pretty negative on the decision, and one person was so admiring and focused on how brave I was to be doing something new and unexpected that it gave her permission to imagine doing something new and possibly outrageous herself.

While I would love for people to think well of me, I can't let that be a guiding factor, and the older I get, the less I care. When you think of the fears and opportunities in your life, take this real-world lesson to heart:

Don't wait for the fear of failure to subside; move forward as if it isn't there.

And keep this picture vividly in mind: You may cringe when you think back to those embarrassing high school memories, but no one remembers them as clearly as you do—they're too busy cringing over their own memories.

Very early in my tenure as a regular expert on *Fast Money*, I really felt like I was in over my head and needed feedback to see how I was doing. The producers were giving me notes, but mostly lots of reassurance. So, with a lack of judgment, perhaps, I sought out comments on the Internet. For the entire first month I was on the air, I surfed Yahoo! Finance and other financial websites and discovered a barrage of commentary about my appearances on the show. I quickly learned that the public hated me and that my performance could be summed up as a disaster. The actual comments were much more colorful, as these choice examples attest:

> *I just figured out who Karen Finerman looks like, she looks like one of Marge Simpson's twin sisters, that stare of hers scares the grease off a kitchen wall!*
> *Is it just me or does that voice of hers just annoy you to death?!?!?!?!*
> *She has the personality of a doorknob.*
> *Get off the show, you are an embarrassment.*

And those are just the ones fit for print. I took the attacks personally.

I remember telling our then-host, Dylan Ratigan, "They

hate me; what do I do?" He had excellent advice: "Never read what they say about you on the Internet. Only the really crazies take the time to write and they always hate everyone. The relatively normal people who either like you or don't feel that strongly don't bother."

That was a great lesson. There was also this:

What other people say about me is none of my business.
—Michael J. Fox

What to do:

- Identify your fear so you can see it and push on anyway.
- Ask yourself whose voice you are listening to. Are you clear about what you want, or do you need to get clear before you solicit advice and opinions that you may be better off ignoring?
- Consider if you are worried about how you "look" or what you can accomplish.
- Work through the risk/reward equation. Is it an asymmetrical risk with the rewards you want? Or is it a risk that isn't important in your big picture?
- Think hard about how you would feel if you succeeded and how you would feel if you didn't try. Practice pushing through your fear instead of waiting or hoping for that fear to subside.

The Failure to Be Proactive

Sometimes opportunities are handed to you, but mostly they're not. If we wait for them, they may never come, or at least not in the way we hoped and to the exact specifications we mapped out in our minds.

In talking about the failure to be proactive, of not stepping up, I'm referring to things like this:

- Waiting to be asked
- Holding yourself back so you don't stand out; underestimating what you can handle and what you might really wish for
- Waiting for an opportunity you can feel really confident about and even overqualified for before taking something on

The failure to be proactive is much worse than you think. It's not just a risk of missing opportunities. It's also a risk of opting out of opportunities and influence that are already yours for the taking. It affects your career, your life (say, in love), your confidence, and your psyche.

I could fill pages of statistics to show how this might affect you, but let me put out two especially vivid examples of this gap, or failure to step up.

In the world of media and politics, one piece of data tells all: A few years ago, an analysis of 654 *Washington Post* op-ed pieces appearing in one six-month period found that 575 published pieces were written by men and 79 by women. That's some differential. But here's the kicker: By a margin of about nine to one, men submitted more op-eds than women. They are in the game. As a woman, as a professional, do you only have something relevant to say one-ninth as many times as men? Or do only one-ninth of women have something to say? This one insight led to the founding of the national

OpEd Project to get more women, diverse voices, and points of view into the public conversations.

In another arena altogether—the world of competitive tennis, where I spent many of my high school years—teenage girls and boys are groomed not only for the highest levels of performance but for winning. Yet a similarly startling discovery was made.

In their book *Getting to 50/50*, Sharon Meers and Joanna Strober tell this story:

> *Beginning in 2006 players at the U.S. Open were allowed to challenge judges on a limited number of line calls, thanks to video replay. When a player challenged a call, the video supported the player's view 30% of the time. This held true whether the player was male or female. So, all players had a strong incentive to challenge calls: 30% of the time they got back a point that they had otherwise lost. You'd think every player would make use of the right to challenge. [But] female athletes, women engaged in one of the most important competitions of their professional lives, challenged calls 1/3 as often as men did.*

Women's leadership expert Tara Sophia Mohr was fascinated with this phenomenon and wrote in her *Wise Living* blog about what it might mean for readers:

> *This little thing that was so closely tied to a point—probably one of the "easiest" things women could do to dramatically transform their careers—they didn't do.*

Male players in the U.S. Open challenged a total of 73 calls. Women challenged only 28. Maybe they, more than the men, assumed that the authority figure—the judge—must have got it right. Maybe they suspected the judges were wrong, but then that flash of concern was overridden by self-doubt. Maybe they felt it would come across as rude or arrogant to question the call, and they wisely reasoned it wouldn't be good for them to question it. Maybe they felt afraid of posing a challenge and being publicly wrong. We don't know why they didn't do it, but of course, something in us knows exactly why they didn't do it. We've been there too.

For Tara Mohr, and for all of us, this begs the question, "Would I be willing to pose public challenges to authority, to the status quo, knowing that about two-thirds of the time I wouldn't 'win the point?'"

Can we change this reality of women challenging the status quo less often than men? What would it take for you to start questioning the calls more frequently, more naturally, more freely? Some of the time, our challenges will miss the mark—they won't be heard. They won't be incorporated. And just as it did for the US Open players, some of the time, our challenges will shift the course of something that matters.

Over and over, we see that women skip over opportunities where they could have influence, make a difference, and even win. As women, we need to see ourselves as leaders and agents of influence and take action on our own behalf. I come back again to the important point because it's worth reiterating. Women think they are faking it when they're not, because most women never feel they are ready.

As individual women, we need to remember that you can't let the risk of failure lead to the very real failure of not being our own best advocates.

What to do:

- Take a look at situations where you haven't spoken on your own behalf this week, this month, this year and consider a way you can take one step to move that conversation forward.
- Be attentive to upcoming opportunities in your work and make a commitment to raise your hand for one of them.
- Think about that one area of business where you *are* an expert—or become that expert—so you proactively make yourself the go-to person people must reach out to.

The Failure to Execute Successfully

The third kind of failure is the one we usually think of. The conventional kind—when you really screw things up—can be devastating, but this kind of tangible and often very-public failure is surmountable and highly likely over the course of our lives. Plus, we can do failure better and reap the benefits. I'm talking about failures like these:

- Not taking the time to do something right the first time
- Not being able to pull off a job or new role (but time can help)
- Losing or not getting a major client or sale when you or the powers that be feel you could have pulled it off

- Not keeping a promise or commitment
- Not showing up when it mattered—literally or figuratively
- Significantly miscalculating—especially when major money, lives, and organizations are at stake

Wherever you are on the failure-to-execute continuum at any given moment, what follows is some unvarnished fessing up and lessons of my own that may help you. If you only take away one thing, let it be that when crisis hits, you can push through it.

The Golden Goose and the Iceberg

My big failure story is of a golden goose and an iceberg, set at my firm, Metropolitan Capital, circa June 1998.

After several spectacular years where it seemed we could do no wrong, we entered 1998 full of bravado and high expectations. In the first six months of the year, Jeffrey and I had negotiated what we thought was an excellent deal. Just six years into our partnership, we were about to sell half our firm at a valuation of about $80 million dollars. This would have given me about $25 million up front *and* continued ownership in the ongoing business, which I imagined would be even more valuable over the coming years. Also, it would have let me wear an imaginary crown that said, "I made it." And on the back it said, "I can pretty much buy whatever I want!"

The deal we struck seemed like it would be the best of both worlds and a win for both parties. We got to keep control of the clients and investments and we could continue to grow without having to become employees of a larger firm.

Our buyers got to jump into a business they didn't have to develop from scratch on their own. The golden goose that was Metropolitan would keep providing for us in *our* venture, and we hoped for *theirs*. The best part was that we still had tremendous upside if we grew.

So there I was at 33, about to make it big and quite impressed with what Jeffrey and I had accomplished. I counted my money over and over in my head, doodled it on notepads, the way a teenage girl might scribble "Mrs. Justin Bieber."

But the disaster-movie music was sounding just offscreen. Only one day before the transaction was supposed to close, the deal fell apart—partly due to our terrible performance in the month prior to the scheduled closing but also due to jitters on the part of our suitors.

Maybe they felt a deep trembling under the surface that wasn't even audible to their ears. Trouble was brewing in the financial world. Something was changing, but we didn't know that yet.

Though we were disappointed at the deal's collapse, I consoled myself with the reality that we had a wildly valuable firm and that maybe—just maybe—we were even better off with no deal. I could savor the chance we might have to sell the company for even more later on or to hang on to it and continue to make more money every year.

So heady were those days that my husband and I purchased a very large "significant" apartment in New York City. I thought I could manage easily with my soon-to-be oh-so-liquid balance sheet or just with the regular gains we were seeing month over month. But, as you might have gathered, disaster struck.

We hit the iceberg—part two of the story. On August 17, 1998, Russia's yearlong financial turmoil took a huge turn for the worse and the country defaulted on its debt. World-wide markets went into a meltdown. Our portfolio went with them.

Let me bring you inside the *Titanic*. That very first day, a Monday, we were losing millions of dollars as every stock we owned in every sector got hit. Things that normally traded in increments of one-eighths and one-fourths (back before the penny spread stocks now trade in) were trading down dollars at a time. Fractions weren't relevant; integers were. I had been through the crash of 1987, but this was different. I was in charge, or at least co–in charge. I didn't even have a chance to think about the millions of dollars that I personally was losing. This went on for days, then weeks.

The calls coming in from "concerned" investors weren't delightful either. I remember one letter from an investor who wanted to withdraw because he'd lost faith in us completely and "couldn't stand one more minute of our horrible performance." We had leaks in our portfolio sprouting from every crevice.

I could scarcely bear to look at the computer screen blinking every time there was a trade in one of our stocks. The news was always bad. I hate violence and bloodshed, and our portfolio made a Tarantino movie look like *Bambi*. Any time the phone rang, my stomach seized. I was fearful that it would be yet another investor wanting to jump ship. Mostly, my fears were borne out. I remember the call from one of our biggest investors, who was traveling in Japan. He had advised a number of large Japanese insurance companies to invest with us. On the call, he said, "Listen, I want to give you a heads-up. They're all going to leave. Every single one." I politely thanked him, but mentally I was throwing up.

Right before our eyes, our portfolio was disintegrating and the business was imploding. As the prices of our holdings were plummeting, we were faced with the inevitable redemptions that come with volatility. Investors would want their money back when they saw how massive the damage to the portfolio was. And we would have to sell things at any price to give them that money back, regardless of what the true value of our holdings was. In the weeks that followed, our analysts were quitting and/or being poached by other firms who smelled blood in the water. Some true friends called with encouraging words about our certain and speedy bounce back. Others, who weren't so true, called to find out the extent of the damage so they could gossip about it, or worse, front-run us—meaning sell stocks they knew we owned because they assumed we would have to sell them to meet withdrawal requests.

Yet through it all, there was one true investor, a substantial one, that I'll always remember. Several of the partners came to meet with us to assess the damage and deliver their verdict: We still believe in you. That one investor (a very large institution in the hedge fund business) had sent us a life preserver. To this day, I am still grateful to them.

After four months of turmoil, the hemorrhaging finally subsided. The market stabilized (helped in part by a surprise rate cut from the Federal Reserve). The trend began to reverse and the market shot upward again, only our shipwreck was still stuck at sea. We had a new influx of cash from the stocks we sold, but we knew we would need that pile of cash to meet year-end redemptions. In the hedge fund world, investors can only withdraw money once a year (often with 90 days' notice), and we couldn't be caught short of cash. As the market quickly regained its losses, this was salt in our wounds. We would finish the year underperforming the market by a stunning 44 percent with no chance to turn things around in the closing weeks.

Because the market had been up so much in the first half of 1998 and the biggest blue-chip, big-name companies like Gillette, Coca-Cola, and P&G were trading at prices we thought were much too expensive and unsustainably high, we chose to focus on small under-the-radar companies that traded at much less expensive metrics—or rather they seemed inexpensive. But nothing was what it seemed. As captains of the ship that year, we did the following:

- **We suffered from extreme hubris.** Up until 1998, we had rarely been wrong. (Perhaps we had been but the strength of the market bailed us out, unbeknownst to us.) It didn't occur to us that we might have made a lot of investing mistakes, not just stocks, which would trade down with the markets, but stocks where our investment thesis was wrong.

- **We had the wrong "hedge" (insurance).** We had built a portfolio of smaller companies ("small caps") but hedged it with "big cap" protection that didn't work at all, because in the panic money flowed to the high-quality, big-cap names and fled the small caps. So rather than neutralizing our losses, our hedge actually made things worse. Our small caps were getting pummeled because there wasn't enough liquidity—that is, buyers—for shareholders who wanted to sell. And the biggest investor who wanted and needed to sell was us. We learned the hard way what happens when you get so big in an investment (those appealing small caps that no one else seemed to be interested in and seemed so cheap) that you become the market. If you want out, the buyers have all the cards. They get to name the price and you have no choice but to accept it, regardless of the underlying perceived value of the investment. So while we thought we were diversified by being in so many different small caps, the reality was we were in one big trade of illiquid, lower-priced, smaller companies that would all trade down together.

- **We didn't know our key customers well enough, or they didn't know us.** We made assumptions that our investors understood and shared our approach, but in hindsight, many of them didn't. It's not simply that they got cold feet or saw a shinier opportunity somewhere else. They really didn't value what we were trying to do. We couldn't convince any of our foreign investors to stick with us, so they all withdrew their money at the end of the year along with many big US institutions.

- **We panicked, somewhat understandably.** Because we didn't know if we would have any investors who would stick with us after the end-of-the-year redemption period, we were filled with fear that we would be short the cash we needed to fulfill those obligations. That would guarantee that we would be wiped out and could ruin our reputations forever. We sold as much as we could at the absolute bottom as 1998 came to a close and held way too much cash as the markets regained all their losses by the end of the year and went on to post stunning gains—which we didn't participate in at all.

And just like that, in six months, we had managed to kill the goose that laid the golden eggs—our goose, the one we worked tirelessly to build and assumed would live forever.

Oh, and then I had that huge apartment—whose renovation costs were skyrocketing over 100 percent above our original budget. I had used nearly all my liquid funds since the building insisted that the apartment itself be paid for 100 percent in cash—no mortgages allowed. Only a loan from Jeffrey gave me any breathing room.

The stress from the collapse of the business and my personal losses was debilitating. One tiny silver lining was that I lost 15 pounds without trying, because I was too devastated to eat.

I had gone from being one of the highest-paid women on Wall Street at 33 years old to being a complete and utter failure. I could hardly look at myself in the mirror. My confidence, my self-esteem, my view of myself in the world were crushed. I didn't know if I could ever bounce back. I had failed in a much bigger and more spectacular way than I had ever thought imaginable. And given how high I was going into it, the fall was that much harder. Ironically, it was one of the best periods of our marriage. Only Lawrence saw how truly shattered I was. I am generally not a crier, but I spent many nights crying and afraid of what would happen next.

I'd gone from thinking I could have purchased anything my heart desired to losing millions of my own money and tens of millions in the value of our business. The thought of the fancy new apartment made me sick. And the massive renovation was just beginning. Demolition—how ironic—had just been completed right in time for me to not want to spend one more penny, let alone millions. I also felt like a fraud.

At some point much later, I was able to clear my head enough to make a list of what I had learned and the mistakes I had made. Yes, I had figured out how to blow up a business. What I also needed to learn was how to be a better investor. I had no better teacher than 1998. If you can learn what you did wrong, then you are a lot closer to getting it right. (In the end, the firm did live on, but it was a journey of many years to get back to solid ground and to rebuild ourselves back up to surpass where we had been at our peak.)

What to do:

- **Don't rest on past performance.** You can learn from your experience, but you can't stop evolving. What worked in one environment may not work in another, so you always need to be testing and pushing yourself.
- **Buy the best company, not the cheapest.** When you buy the cheapest and you are getting a perceived "value," you are likely giving up something extremely important like market position, pricing power, a good management team, or balance-sheet strength. This will cost you dearly in the end. Those "small caps" we owned were cheap for a reason. In everything you buy that matters—whether it's a new printer, a new set of knives, or a new hire—pick quality over price. You'll always have something of greater value, and in the end it may cost you less.

- **Recognize when you have too much ego invested in a position and have lost perspective.** This point can apply to your whole-life perspective or to real-life minutiae, such as what your kids wear to school. Did you punt and choose law school only to realize you hated it and didn't want to be there? Deep down you know it's not for you. Cut your losses. No matter how much you may wish and even will something to work out, facing the reality that you are wrong and need to get out of a position is what you need to do.

  Interestingly, I find that women are far, far better at this than men. Studies have shown that women are better investors. One of the more interesting of those studies showed that two women together make the best investment team, followed by a male/female pair; in last place is the pair of men. Women do not suffer from the same hubris that might make men afraid to admit defeat while there is still time to do something about it. In addition, women trade around their positions less and therefore save on fees and the cost of not having that perfect market timing that men like to believe they have.

  These are huge points. Selling a stock for a small loss is often the very best trade you can make. Fixing a mistake sooner rather than later makes losses smaller and the recovery faster: Nearly every big money loser we've ever had started out as a small money loser.

- **Be very skeptical when you listen to management's rosy projections.** Management teams are usually made up of at least one person, likely the CEO who is a real optimist and people person. He'll (and sadly, 95-plus times out of 100 this person is a man) express excitement about his business and its prospects, and I'll become convinced of the bull case for the stock. The teams that underpromise and overdeliver are harder to come by. That's who I want to invest in. Most of the time, though, the CEO is a charming champion of his company and its stock. How can this apply to the non–hedge fund manager? Did you ever interview a contractor for a renovation? A painter? They will often tell you what you want to hear about costs and timing, hoping you'll choose them and they'll deal with your frustration, time, and cost overruns later. If every other painter quotes a time frame of three to four weeks except one who says 10 days, be skeptical.

- **Never get yourself in the position of having investments with a long-term horizon when you have investors who only care about short-term performance.** If they want out, you have to give up control of when you buy and sell to someone else. You never want to give up control. Better to know your investors and clients and for them to know you—eyes wide open from the outset. Be clear to yourself. Is your boyfriend a fling versus a long-term commitment? Do you have a placeholder job but you're staying with it out of fear of change?

- **Understand precisely what you own and see what inadvertent risks you may be taking on.** For example, some companies have risks imbedded in them that don't appear to the naked eye. Let's pick a simplified example. Say you want to invest in Tupperware because you like their products and think in this economically depressed environment more people will cook and eat at home and will need Tupperware-type products. Be aware, you may also be making the bet that oil won't trade too high—a

key component in plastic—therefore the costs to manu-
facture Tupperware may spiral out of control. What else
might you be accidentally betting on, and can you accept that risk? What about the boyfriend who never has
a sense of responsibility—would you be comfortable being the sole breadwinner?

- **Invest sufficiently in the business to have it grow at critical points.** This was extremely shortsighted. I didn't
want to spend money on expanding staff—specifically,
hiring a professional CFO when we really needed one. I
couldn't justify spending the money, but I was wasting
too much of my time on things that I really wasn't
properly trained to do (and hated—and did a bad job
executing) and not spending enough time on things that
would improve the business—a pre-1998 lesson but an
important one, nonetheless.

- **Learn something from each failure.** The danger in failure
isn't just in the failure itself. Awful as that can be, it's
survivable. It's in not learning the lessons from it. I try
to go over every bad investment I ever made. What went
wrong? Why? Was there an error in my decision-making
process? Sometimes you've made a wise decision based
on all the information you had available to you at that
time, but it just didn't work out. If you make enough
investments, the law of averages will force such an occurrence, but be sure you are not overlooking something
you did wrong. Conversely, sometimes you get lucky and
make money when you had no business doing so, when
your decision-making was faulty.

- **Don't blame someone else for your mistakes.** My favorite
thing about my partner, Jeffrey, is that he is the last guy

to take credit for success and the first guy to take blame for mistakes. In the case of disappointing projects, taking the blame means you proactively say, "I am not going to meet the quarter, here's why, and here's what I propose we do about it," or "I blew it, I dropped the ball, and now I will try to fix it." Taking blame can start to neutralize a problem. There is no more time wasted on finger pointing and disagreement. The focus becomes solely on a solution. Plus, you will gain the respect of others in your organization for taking blame actively if, in fact, it should fall on your shoulders. Those moments can become lore for years and can win you many supporters.

If I think back to the day in front of that group of Wharton students, I realize how little they knew and how little we can prepare for the really hard times. We can—and must—learn by watching. Our curiosity can help us enormously. But our blind spots are there till we bump into things.

If we survive failure, we haven't failed—we've learned and we've grown stronger, scars and all.

Failures in my book aren't the mistakes and the disappointments—as monumental as they are sometimes. Failures are those times we let fear and a refusal to see and take blame for our mistakes prevent our ability to bounce back. If you can develop resilience and learn from your failures, then a failure can become a journey worth taking and a triumph in the end.

CHAPTER 7

Take the Path of Most Resilience

Character cannot be developed in ease and quiet. Only through experience of trial and suffering can the soul be strengthened, ambition inspired, and success achieved.
—Helen Keller

Make your bed every day. I didn't ask whether you felt like it.   —Jane (Mom) Finerman

It's happened. The thing you feared. Failure. It's as jarring as that time in school when you may have actually gotten an F. Maybe there was a little note in red felt-tip that said, "See me." Your stomach drops and tears well up in your eyes.

Now you're a grown-up and you feel that mark of failure again. It's scary. It's stunning—literally. You actually feel frozen and in pain, while adrenaline courses through your veins. You mentally seize up. You might feel unable to function.

For me, the near-death destruction of our business was like a scarlet letter F that was embroidered on my psyche—and that I was sure showed on my chest as well. It was paralyzing and all-encompassing. I never thought I would get past it. At 33, I was done, the best of my career behind me, and I felt like everyone knew it, too.

For my friend Janet, it was the realization that her marriage was over and she would in all likelihood become a single mom. I remember the tearful dinner. She's generally a crier, but this was different. She only half-jokingly said, "Well, if it's just Ruby [her daughter] and Charmaine [the babysitter] and me, we can make it." When upper middle-class Jewish girls imagine themselves as single mothers, they envision a threesome: mom and kid and nanny. That thinnest thread of hope and camaraderie was her only sense of a lifeline—and a sense of humor that allowed her to laugh at her situation as easily as she could cry. There is no non-life-threatening situation so bad where having a sense of humor does not make it better, if even for only a moment.

For another friend, Lisa—who "knew" she was on the verge of getting fired for a year (she saw the writing on the wall the day a standard business trip wasn't approved)—it was the panic that her identity was getting pulled out from under her. Her career had been devoted to changing lives, and yet she felt despair about changing hers in the face of the crisis; she felt she might never find work that mattered—or any work—again.

This is the moment on which success is built—not the victories, the winning, the momentum, or the luck. It is in this moment that you will decide what you are made of and what your character truly is. It won't be easy; don't expect it to be. It will take all your strength to act and move forward. It will take all your wisdom and maturity to be patient. The road back is both immediate (there are things you can and must do right now) and long (the journey that will change you and heal you will take time). Get on with it.

Five Steps to Getting On with It

So what's the plan? When major disappointment arrives, when the sh_t hits the fan, here's mine:

1. Fake it—play hurt and get back in the game.
2. Plot your future—set incremental, achievable goals.
3. Recalibrate—think anew and act on what matters.
4. Revisit—get a fresh view and perspective.
5. Change it up—do daily things that give you a fresh start.

Fake It—Play Hurt and Get Back in the Game

This is perhaps the most important step because it's the first one. It's the reaction phase to the failure. It's when you tell yourself that you can recover. Do not give yourself the expansive, unrestricted room nor the luxury to wallow. You may give yourself a tiny amount of defined time for slovenly self-indulgence—a weekend maybe of sweatpants, not showering, tears, and ice cream—but that's it. I know that the pain won't be over in a weekend, but the full-time wallowing must be. A defined, contained bit of self-pity won't kill you, but that's it. Then move onward.

You can't wait to feel good or strong or confident. In spite of everything, you have to get out there and create a new normal. It won't feel comfortable at first, but that's not the point. For God's sake, we're women. How many things have we faked in our lives? In particular, if you're a manager or leader, face your team. They need to see that you haven't gone to pieces. They are looking at you for direction. If you're younger or less senior, do the same by putting on a "public face" at the office. It's not dishonest to show grace and poise and that you're a grown-up who can figure things out. You don't need to know the path back right away. But you need to show that this isn't going to take you down.

My husband and I used to laugh about the spin control we did with our children when they were little. For example, if they fell and hurt themselves, there was this split second when they would look at us to gauge how big a deal the injury was and therefore how they should react. Assuming there wasn't a tremendous amount of blood, we used to say, "OK, OK; you're OK," or "You silly goose, you're so funny," or something equivalent and then literally pop them upright immediately.

Your team and the people around you are looking at you for the grown-up version of that. It doesn't mean you should pretend nothing happened. Address the issue, but don't give yourself permission to fall apart. Damage control isn't just for the outside world. It's for you, too. Falling apart is for tragedies and deaths—not for failures. You need to have your best "I can make it; I've got this under control" demeanor for the outside world.

You don't need to fake it all the time or to everyone. You need a confidant to whom you can reveal how bad you really feel. That confidant can be a best friend, a spouse, a therapist, a lawyer, your mom—anyone who is on your side and with whom you feel safe enough to show your vulnerabilities. That opportunity to vent will allow you to recharge your batteries when you have to go out and put your game face back on. It's fine that the confidant knows you're faking it. The right people will not see your failure as insurmountable, and they will want to be there for you. Just think about how you've been that confidant to someone else. Let someone be that person for you.

Plot Your Future—Set Incremental, Achievable Goals

Even if you only have a tiny bit of energy each day to think and plan, you need to create a road map of how you are going to make your way back. The act of sitting down and addressing both where you are and where you want to get (back) to is in itself proactive and productive. Do it.

It's OK to set small goals at first, even if they are timid. They can help you get your vision and confidence back. Also, you need to be realistic. Most failures of significance cannot be righted immediately. It's possible, of course, but not likely. If you've lost a promotion or an election, another one won't just magically appear.

For me, with the devastating collapse of our firm's investments in 1998, the road map was for us just to stop losing investors. Our first goal was not to grow, not to make it all back. That came much later.

Break down your next steps and goals into small pieces. Win one piece of business. Find one new good investment. Build one new partnership. Meet people, set up interviews, take time to really consider the right next roles and positions, initiate an interim project. Near-term goals that are achievable are important because the bigger, longer-term goals can take years.

Recalibrate—Think Anew and Act on What Matters

For the really large failures, you need to look hard at all parts of your life to help find a way out and to recalibrate your identity and some of your goals. If it's comforting to spend some time with family, then do it. Find what centers you. If you've spent the last 10 years focused on being made a division president and you've just lost the promotion, your internal compass will spin out of control. This was your goal line for years and now you have to pretend it doesn't matter. Something else must matter to you also, even if that something else doesn't jump out at you right away. Recalibrate to focus on that something else—perhaps temporarily, perhaps permanently. You don't need to know which time frame that is right now. You just need something firm and steady to hold on to until the storm passes. Then you can assess the damage.

For me, not spending money was a way to start to feel in control. Even though I had big expenses at just the moment in my life when I experienced my biggest failure, I felt I could control some of my everyday spending. I walked everywhere. I only bought things on sale. I didn't spend time looking for things to fill our new apartment. Anything that used to remind me of how flush I had felt about money became something to avoid. Even if the dollars saved didn't change the overall picture, in some weird way, they gave me some feeling of control.

Revisit—Get a Fresh View and Perspective

This step is something that may be easier to implement than others because it's so concrete. However, its true worth is only seen sometime down the road. Right after the failure occurs, take some time to write down exactly how you're feeling. The more descriptive and horrible the details, the better. Include anecdotes to really paint the picture of how bad this failure feels and how deeply it hurts you, regardless of whether it's a failed relationship or a major work failure. (The writing in itself may be cathartic, but it's not my main point.)

Then, pick a time to revisit this description and see how you feel at that future date versus how badly you feel now. Six months may be enough time. You want to give your failure—and your natural resilience—a little time to breathe. The bigger the failure, the further out it should be.

I think about doing this for my children when they face their first big heartaches in the hope that after the allotted time expires and they see how much better they feel, they will believe me when I tell them that "this, too, shall pass." Think of your own examples right now of how time healed some painful wounds. It could be a first love who you thought you'd die without or a first job where you knew you were terrible and had no idea what you were doing, and you extrapolated from there to believe you would never be able to hold any meaningful job ever.

While this step doesn't help right away, once you've done both parts (the writing and the later rereading) and have seen how effective it is, you will know for the next time how resilient you really can be.

Change It Up—Do Daily Things that Give You a Fresh Start

Whatever steps you're able to manage, slowly but surely things will shift. But often there's an invisible hazy, dark cloud that you sense is surrounding you, and it colors everything—not in a good way.

You're going to need to do something to make you feel at least a little bit different than the awful aura of failure lets you feel. Even a small change can make a difference. Actually, a smallish change is better. This is not the time to make broad, far-reaching decisions in an effort to escape where you are. I'm talking about practical things like joining a gym, buying some new bedding, getting a fresh haircut (not a Mohawk), or taking on a new hobby.

My first big depression, before the 1998 fiasco, was in my 20s. The LBO boom had gone bust, the stock market was tanking, and things had gone terribly wrong at the firm where I worked. (That was the time of the UAL debacle, which hit us very hard.) I knew something bad was coming. I sensed that the firm would soon fold, and I would be out of a job. Wall Street was turning out to be far more treacherous than glamorous. I was worried that I was about to get kicked out of an industry that I had dreamed of being part of since I was a teenager.

For the first time, I was facing an uncertain future with no preordained path ahead of me. I had very little money saved, and having to move home, back to California, would have been a total defeat. It was proving so difficult to keep panic at bay.

With activity at the office slowing to a trickle, the vast expanse of free time that awaited me nightly was unbearable. I had to do something—anything—to fill it. Maybe, I thought, I could do something I had been wanting to do for a long time. Something that would give me some tiny sense of accomplishment while trying not to fall into the abyss of failure. I decided I would learn how to draw. (What? You were expecting skydiving?)

I bought the book *Drawing on the Right Side of the Brain*,

which promised, right on the cover, that it could teach anyone how to draw. Diligently, I went through the chapters, one each night. I really did learn how to draw, and to this day I am able to sketch silly drawings at restaurant tables when we go to establishments that serve large drinks and have crayons on the table, much to my kids' delight (though they are outgrowing their appreciation for any marginal talents I might have, and thankfully we go to a lot fewer restaurants with crayons). Perhaps I should have learned French, but the point remains. Do something.

* * *

It was also about that time that I began to work out. It was another simple thing I could do to feel that I could accomplish something at will. I didn't have to wait for something good to happen to me. Twenty-five years later, I haven't stopped my workout regimen.

Daily activities come in all shapes and sizes. As Gretchen Rubin, the wonderful author of *The Happiness Project*, discovered (and this is for real), when you make your bed in the morning, you feel better for the whole day. It turns out our mothers were right.

Try it. It's one thing you can accomplish while taking care of yourself in a small way at the same time.

Learn from It—Get Honest and Find the Lessons

There will come a moment when you can bear the pain of looking at what happened. You can go over the events without triggering your personal cocktail of remorse, shame, embarrassment, or anger.

Whether in small increments, or when you're really ready to take a full look at the lessons you can learn, it's important to ask yourself what happened. When I make investing mistakes, I review the following:

- Was there an error in my decision-making process or was the failure in part due to the law of averages? As I mentioned in chapter 4, if you make enough investments, enough decisions or recommendations, sometimes they will not work out. But you always have to be sure you're not overlooking something you did wrong. Conversely, sometimes you get lucky and make money when you had no business doing so, when your decision making was faulty.
- When and how did you pretend a potential problem wasn't there?
- Did you miss seeing a coming change in the environment—whether in the marketplace, the people around you, the pulse of what was going on?
- Were you honest with yourself about what was working and what wasn't?
- Were you thinking ahead about what you wanted and where you were going?
- Did you realize at some point along the way that there was a problem but chose to ignore it?

The idea here isn't to be hard on yourself or to go through a litany of what ifs. It's to help you see what you can control and what you can do differently.

Also, this idea of learning the lessons isn't about comparing your success—or your failure—to others. It's about learning who you are and becoming better. As destabilizing as it is to make mistakes, it is also empowering to see pitfalls you've learned to avoid. I have a sense of accomplishment when I see an investment gone wrong that we weren't in. I say to myself, "That was a rookie mistake," and I take a little pride in the hard-earned lessons I have learned.

If I can't use a failure or disappointment to any positive effect, then I'm just wasting my time. If I can, then I'm stronger, wiser, and a lot more fun to be around.

Resilience at Metropolitan Capital

Back at the office, business had to go on at Metropolitan Capital. Beyond the personal aspect of getting to the other side of our epic losses, there was the business aspect of actually getting from where we were to wherever we were going next.

After the dust settled and my partner, Jeffrey, and I could review the extensive, obliterating damage of 1998, we knew we had to rebuild. Giving up was not an option. We have this expression: You don't get stupid overnight. What it means is that you can make mistakes, and things can move against you, but you likely still have some skills. And while I felt stupid, I hadn't instantaneously become so. We had a skill set. We could rebuild, though my hopes—fantasies, really—for a quick fix faded almost immediately when we surveyed the extent of the damage.

We had clients who left, including large institutional investors who took years to cultivate and who would likely never return, a team that was devastated, and tens of millions of dollars of losses to dig out from. The whole task seemed so daunting and impossible.

The first step was faking it. I had to pretend to myself, our staff, those clients who wisely and thankfully stuck with us, and the outside world of Wall Street and beyond that we would come back from this. We needed to project to everyone that our turnaround wasn't an *if* but merely a *when* (even though I wasn't quite convinced myself).

Every morning I arrived at the office just a little bit earlier than I used to in order to show myself, mainly, that I was going to work even harder and be even more focused than I was before. We had lost our way in our success and now we were going to find it back in our failure.

Meanwhile, I plotted the future—literally. I mapped out the small incremental wins we'd need month over month in earnings, new investments, and new clients to get back to where we were. These concrete tasks were extremely reassuring. I was doing something specific. I was breaking it down and working the plan. I guesstimated how long it was going to take and revised those estimates monthly. In some ways, I'm glad that I underestimated how long it would take to rebuild, because if I'd known, I might have been overwhelmed by the task. Focusing on the little, immediate things was helpful emotionally, and it was effective, too. I do the same thing on any big projects I have today.

Yet the reality couldn't be escaped. An instant bounce back wasn't going to happen. The fact was we had underperformed the market dramatically. When everyone else was up big, we were down. The damage was too great. I had to break down our goal as well. We had to rethink what success meant. First, we had to make back all the losses for the investors who stayed with the fund. If they had $10 million in the fund and we lost approximately 20 percent in our portfolio of investments, then we needed to earn back 25 percent on the remaining $8 million, or $2 million, to make them whole to where they were at the beginning of 1998. That's just the way the math works. (Losing 20 percent on $10 million means you've lost $2 million and the remaining funds are worth $8 million, but you need to earn back 25 percent gains on that $8 million to get back to $10 million.)

This concept is called "new high ground." It's important because as fund owners, we don't get paid—meaning we don't start taking our fees—until we start making gains *above* this new high ground. So before we could begin to earn money again (not just earnings on the money we personally had invested in the funds, which were substantial), we had to get everyone back to new high ground. No matter how smart we were, it was going to take more than a few months to get us there.

Only then could we focus on rebuilding the business to where it was before the disaster. That is, only then could we really focus on bringing in significant new clients and additional investments.

As we went from a mode of surveying the damage to the rebuilding phase, I felt energized. At least we were moving forward, not backward. We had survived the horrific losses, the hedges gone awry, the pain of sitting on cash to meet future withdrawals while the market shot to new highs. Mercifully though, the annus horribilis came to an end. While money never sleeps, like the tagline in *Wall Street* says, the end of each calendar year does give you a chance for renewal. The "game" begins again, and you revisit your portfolio with fresh eyes.

This is a really important point. You buy your portfolio

every day, meaning the only relevant price for everything you own is where it is marked currently. It doesn't matter whether you bought it higher or lower; all that matters is whether you want to own it right now at this price. We got rid of what we really didn't believe in and put the mistakes behind us.

I scribbled some notes about what I learned in this period and have kept the scratchy little torn piece of paper I wrote them on to this day. The one I've turned to the most is this (the salty language is leftover from my time on the DLJ trading floor): "Don't dick for an 1/8." (At that time, stocks traded in one-eighths of a dollar, or 12.5-cent increments; now they trade in pennies.)

When I wrote this down, I didn't mean for anyone but me to see it, so pardon the language but not the message. For me, this one little phrase carries a wealth of meaning. First:

Don't belabor a transaction for a small amount of money. If you want to sell something, get out there and sell it. Don't try to squeeze every last penny.

Next:

If it's not what you thought, sell it.

This means don't create a reason why you should still own a stock even though your original thesis is wrong. It's liberating to sell your losers.

And the last thing, which has never been truer than in the last few years, is this:

Markets can change very quickly. Do not extrap-olate well into the future what the environment is right now.

Markets are a metaphor for life—jobs, relationships, physical well-being. It can all change so quickly, and you will find it hard to remember how it used to be. I've thought about this several times in my marriage when we hit rough patches of distance from each other and irritability when we each feel the other just doesn't appreciate us. Being married is hard, but no one tells you that. The best advice I ever got about marriage was from the CEO of the big institutional firm that stuck with us after 1998. She said that marriage isn't about good days and bad days, but about good years and bad years. I know those tough periods will end.

Thinking in terms of a clean slate was helpful to my psy-che and the company's. I had to break out of the despair that was never far off and my view of myself as a colossal failure. With our activity, planning, and re-visioning of our goals into something achievable, I started thinking of myself as someone who was rebuilding toward what I believed would be eventual success rather than someone who was a failure.

In the end, it took us just six months to make back our losses for our clients that stayed. That was nice, but 1999 was a good year for everyone. We didn't get to really show our true skills as investors again until 2000. However, it would take us nearly five years to get our fund back to the size we were, and that came from getting many new in-vestors. Each new account or new investor was a minor (or major) victory, and I so appreciated every single one. Any fu-ture success would be that much sweeter.

As the clouds started to part and the haze began to lift, there was a huge opportunity for redemption that was building. It was slow at first, too vague to make out right away. The year 1999 proved to be a stellar one in the markets, and we had a spectacular year even far over and above the markets in general. Everything worked, meaning we made money on just about every investment we made. But we couldn't take too much credit. Just about everybody made money that year. The economy was humming. The technology bubble was starting to expand. The Internet was changing the way business was done. Stocks overall began to reflect the ebullience.

As the bubble grew from 1999 to 2000, market participants and pundits began to speak of a new paradigm for companies. Anytime a company put out a press release that mentioned the Internet or telecommunications, their stock would jump wildly. We could not believe how ridiculous this was getting. We knew we were witnessing a massive mania in the making.

Avoiding the Internet Bubble

We're value investors at our firm, which means we try to find value in companies the market may have discarded, dismissed, or overlooked. Often we gravitate to things that may be currently out of favor, yet we believe they could be back in favor again one day or quite soon, or maybe they just need a little fixing up. We think about what could be and how a company could realistically get there, not what its financials may look like right now. We know that market participants tend to overreact and to extrapolate the reality of today far into the future. For example, the idea that home ownership is a good thing is hardly in fashion, yet I believe this is the best time to buy a home in more than a generation. We are interested, therefore, in what is decidedly out of fashion.

Most of us like to feel that we are fashionable, that we look good in what we wear, and that we can change with the times. For me, I used to see a new trend, think, "I'd never wear that," and only come around to it when it's just about over. Then I'd look sort of passé. Though as I've gotten older, I know more about what works for me, what I want to highlight, and what I want to hide. I can flirt with a trend, but I can't play dress-up in someone else's clothes or someone else's personality. I try to invest with that same thought in mind.

One of our finest moments as a firm was during that time when the Internet was going mainstream and the possibilities seemed endless.

In 1999, the sector that nobody could get enough of—namely, dot-coms—was actually, in our view, the emperor's new clothes. The priceless, never-before-seen garments were manufactured on Wall Street and in Silicon Valley and were for sale everywhere. Here's how the process worked.

Wall Street was feeding the frenzy. New technology companies needed funding to build their businesses. Wall Street would fund those businesses by selling shares to the public, often in an IPO, or initial public offering. The best customers of the Wall Street firms would be able to buy those shares on the IPO and then sell them, literally the next day, for vastly more than they paid.

Every day investors threw money at Internet stocks and at

technology mutual funds to get in on the scheme. The more money there was chasing the stocks, the higher they went. Further fueling this bubble was an unrestrained optimism about how the Internet would forever revolutionize business. How could you put a fair price on companies such as this?

Apparently, in this new world there was no way to measure how potentially valuable this new way of business could be. Old metrics of measuring fundamental cash flow and assets of a business were seen as old school and irrelevant. There were new metrics to be learned, like "eyeballs." The number of eyeballs that looked at a site was a must-know metric. Then you multiply the number of eyeballs by some crazy number (whose genesis was always a mystery to me) to get a valuation for a stock. It didn't matter if the company could make any revenue off the number of eyeballs or not. I always wondered if each person represented one eyeball or two, but it didn't really seem to matter. "If you weren't onboard and investing in Internet stocks, then you just didn't get it" was the mantra of one of the most famous Internet investors of the day, Alberto Vilar. (He was later imprisoned for fraud despite his claims that he was innocent. He is seeking an appeal of his conviction.)

It seemed that there was nothing that could stop this bubble—perhaps it wasn't a bubble, but a revolution like the Industrial Revolution of the United States in the early twentieth century. Perhaps the gravitational pull of the earth would no longer be relevant either.

Not far from the site of the original Gold Rush near San Francisco in 1849, Silicon Valley was the new mecca. Techies headed there in droves to seek their fortunes starting new companies and finding their gold. Wall Street banks were falling all over themselves to get in good with the techies. Goldman Sachs ran an ad in the *Wall Street Journal* showing all their employees dressed in khakis to demonstrate that they could "connect" to the new generation.

If you didn't know how to start a technology company, you could just trade stocks in technology companies. People all over the United States were quitting their jobs to become day traders. And why not? You could make far more money doing that than you could being employed in the Old World economy. You didn't need to understand what the company did, how they did it, or how they could ever make money. Even seasoned corporate executives were quitting their jobs to join start-ups with only stock options as compensation (which seemed just as good as millions of dollars).

There didn't seem to be a job or industry that wasn't cashing in on the Internet bubble. There were even specialized financial planners to help those dealing with the stress of becoming wildly wealthy overnight at a very young age. Who needs that stress?

The mania was feeding on itself. I remember one company, Pets.com, which became a darling because it was going to sell pet supplies over the Internet. This wasn't just pet food—it was Internet pet food. What could be better? In addition, they had a clever mascot—the sock puppet. The puppet was appealing with the tagline PETS.COM: BECAUSE PETS CAN'T DRIVE. They milked that puppet for all it was worth, even buying a Super Bowl ad in 2000. The company represented by a sock puppet became worth several hundred million dollars after the IPO, even though the business was actually losing money—a lot of money. Turns out it's really expensive to ship bags of kibble to each customer.

We at Metropolitan Capital didn't get it. We didn't understand how decades of corporate finance theory could be turned on its ear and found to be totally irrelevant. How could it *not* matter if companies could ever make money? How could the market pay such crazy valuations for companies that didn't even exist two years earlier? These weren't cures for cancer. And how could people so dumb make this much money in Internet stocks? These companies had no assets, no functional business models, no strategic advantage, and 22-year-old college dropouts at their helms. This euphoria went against everything we hold dear as value investors. We just couldn't see it. We were at first bemused, then frustrated, then furious.

Some of our investors questioned why we didn't feel inclined to jump on the bandwagon. We were at times briefly tempted to jump in, because it seemed so easy. But in the end, we weren't swayed.

We looked elsewhere. Not surprisingly, we were finding that great businesses with real earnings power and real assets but with no obvious connection to the Internet were left for dead. Value gold mines like industrial companies and insurance companies were trading at the cheapest metrics we had ever seen, yet no one cared. These stocks weren't sexy; there was no sizzle. Yet we knew they had enduring value.

Our portfolio was the fashion equivalent of socks with sandals. But American industry still needed supplies, and the financial system still had to function. Old, boring businesses weren't shutting down. We stood our ground. As a student of the market, I'd read about panic and euphoria beginning with the Dutch tulipomania to the robber barons to the crash of '29. I'd seen how markets could disconnect from reality. It's just impossible to know for how long. In the spring of 1999, the technology space started to suffer some cracks under the weight of its own size. There was no more money left to be sucked into the mania. Yet the last players to arrive just couldn't believe they had missed the party. There was a brief rally that fall, but then the biggest mania the world had ever seen crumbled.

We saw fortunes lost, jobs lost, and life savings wiped out. Stocks that had traded for hundreds of dollars per share fell to single digits. Companies losing 90 percent or more of their market value were not uncommon. As investors finally fled the sector, there was no one left to sell the stocks to except at prices in the pennies and dollars, so some investors just hung on. Hope springs eternal; stock valuations don't. Exactly 268 days after their IPO, Pets.com liquidated. The stock, which had a market value in the hundreds of millions of dollars, went to $0 (though the licensing rights to the sock puppet were later purchased for a few hundred thousand dollars).

The Internet bubble and the fortunes of Metropolitan Capital taught me how things change over time. So what do you think the lessons were for us? After a failure, it would have been easy to have our convictions shaken and been tempted to chase the new hot thing, but that would have spelled disaster. We had to remain true to the part of us that was valuable and rethink and rebuild the parts that were not.

As rational minds prevailed, the companies that had been left for dead were now seen as extraordinary values, and money flowed to them. For 2000, when the market was down 9.10 percent, we were up 26.48 percent. It was the biggest single year of outperformance we've ever had. We knew who we were. Redemption was ours, finally.

* * *

When I relive all that happened and what I learned from that fall when our firm came close to collapse, I recognize that the scar is still there, and it will always be. Even though we ultimately rebuilt entirely and ended up far past that point of our prior peak, I still retain a little bit of the humbling sense of shock and loss. It's always there—I've just learned to live with it.

But I also never forget that I got through it. And the funny thing is, I've had to think back hard to remember the details of what happened. I had forgotten many of the specific wounds—the sale of the company that fell through, the investment mistakes, the investors who left, our management shortfalls. But I am still very much in touch with the feeling that everything can crumble.

Some scars heal completely and fully, like the pain of infertility that ended with the joy of four children. Scars fade though the feelings and lessons stay. I also know for certain that more failure awaits (and more resilience, I trust). So be it.

As you cope and muddle through with your own failures, whatever their scale, be gentle with yourself, but take action. Resilience is a martial art—perhaps calm on the outside, but fierce on the inside. You can get there. You must get there.

Onward. It is the only path you can take.

CHAPTER 8

Be Where You Are

Be where you are is not as Zen as it sounds. I only arrived at this philosophy after exhausting every other possible route. I just wish it hadn't taken me so long.

After college, all I could think about was being further along in my career. I worried that I wouldn't be the success I hoped to be. Then I started to worry about never finding the right guy, then about having kids, then about . . .

Ironically, worrying about how everything would turn out didn't help me seize the moment. It did the opposite.

While thinking ahead *is* good, it's not everything. For any football fan, one of the most frustrating moments of a game is when the receiver turns to head down the field before he's fully caught the pass—as he tries to think about turning the reception into greater yardage—but then drops the ball. He ends up with nothing—no reception, no gain, and a wasted down. I speak often about taking the long view, thinking ahead, imagining what might come next. Sometimes, though, you just have to get the first part done. Worry about getting the extra yardage after you've secured the ball.

Each stage of life, each goal, each turning point is worth

savoring. Always wanting to be somewhere else means you miss the very essence of where you are, and even who you are at that time. Especially with our personal lives, being in the moment can sometimes be the only and best way through.

From finding love, choosing marriage, and making a family to taking on that fraught label "working mom" and figuring out that you really can't be two places at once, we can train ourselves to get all we can out of each of those moments. We're not born knowing these things, but we can learn and practice them.

Be Where You Are for the Single Girl

One of the biggest mistakes I made during my single years was this: When I was not at the office working late, I was not being a young, on-the-town twentysomething in New York City. I really did want to meet someone and have a relationship and get married. Yet for many years, I never did anything to make it happen.

I'd work hard and skip the office hallway conversations and pizza and beer on Thursday evenings. A few nights a week I'd head to the gym and would work out with metaphorical blinders on, and I would head back to my apartment for dinner, alone. I never put myself in situations where I would meet anyone.

I had made myself totally unavailable, though I certainly didn't see it that way. I had some misguided sense that if it was meant to be, it would just happen. The obstacles I put in the way were like a dare: "If you love me, you'll find me" seemed to be my very poor strategy.

Of course, there are no guarantees that if you put yourself out there, Mr. Right will be just around the corner, but the odds are certainly better than if you just stay home. *Be where you are* means letting yourself be at work, be in solitude, and be connected to others. No definition of success, however, includes isolation, stoicism, or takeout five nights a week (unless your dream is to marry General Tso). *Be where you are* means playing when it's time to play, unplugging when it's time to unplug.

I sometimes had trouble making the transition and would hide at work to avoid the loneliness of being alone. Deep down I knew what I was doing but would rationalize it by telling myself how hard I was working and how impossible my job was. This may sound counter to a point I will make about office face time. I fully believe you need to be at work. My point is to be in the office when it's time for that and to not be there when it isn't. You know the difference.

If I had to do it over (assuming I would still meet Lawrence), I would have been out and about a lot more in my 20s, which doesn't have to mean a designated stool at a local bar. I would have been getting involved in things, going out with groups of friends, improving my odds, experiencing new things. Just as you need to create the opportunity for chance encounters at work, so, too, do you need to do it in your social life.

There was no online dating when I was single, but if I were single now, I'd be on several websites. I've heard every negative comment about them, including, "I don't know why a guy who is 5'4" would say he's 5'10"; is he hoping I'm bad at math? How long does he think he can hide this?" But still, I'd do it anyway. I know too many people who have met someone great online to ever rule it out. It takes work to be visible—it's hard, and you're taking risks, but it is so much better than being invisible.

Be honest with yourself about where you are and why. Remember this:

I never met anyone in my apartment, and neither will you.

I realized that the hunt for my Superman would have to take place outside of my starter one bedroom. I allowed myself to be set up on a few dates, including a blind date arranged by my favorite aunt, Adele—the one who always remembered my birthday, sent cards for my high school and college graduations, and just seemed to be that family person you could always rely on for a thoughtful call or bit of encouragement. It so happened that a friend from her temple whom she played bridge with had a single son in New York City, and well, I was single in New York City—that should be enough for a match, no?

In Aunt Adele's defense, she had met her friend's son and knew he was friendly, funny, and smart, and she also knew I didn't necessarily know what was good for me in this arena.

Adele: Karen, I have someone for you to go out with.
Me: That's very nice of you, but I don't know.
Adele: Trust me, he's good. He's smart and funny and a wonderful son.
Me (*thinking*): Wonderful son—sounds like he's in love with his mother.

To say I was hesitant is an understatement. We met for a drink—the mutually imposed constraint—so we'd both have a fast excuse to keep it short if there were no sparks, or worse. Much to our surprise, we had plenty to talk about, thanks to the icebreaker provide by our "meddling" relatives, and swapped stories of how we'd been talked into this date in the first place. I actually wished we had allotted a bit more time for the evening. I was just so shocked that Aunt Adele could have set me up with someone so great. We dated for a month or so; I really enjoyed his company, wit, and easygoing gentle manner. But in the end, we had that "nice person, not *the one*" feeling. However, those few dates got me going. It was refreshing to be out on the town on weekend nights. It inspired me to keep trying. I do run into him from time to time and always have such fond feelings.

Then came the plagues—frogs, locusts, and *there's a reason this guy is still single*. Once people knew I was "available"—some signal I hadn't let show before—introductions came pouring in from friends, friends of friends, and my own making. There was the bodybuilder / Wall Street guy who was far prettier than I would ever be; the total goofball / fraternity brother with a good heart and a penchant for Cheetos who invited me to play Frisbee (fun) on our first and only date; the too-cool-for-me soccer stud who ended up years later working in our office; the Napoleon look-alike, a master of the universe (his own), who I learned fell to pieces when Drexel Burnham went under; the guy in my building with whom I had a friends-with-benefits arrangement and whom I referred to with my girlfriends as Laundry Room Guy. We'd do our dirty wash together in the basement, and while the clean clothes were drying downstairs, we'd go upstairs to take our now-sweaty clothes off. But still, there wasn't "the one."

I was searching and searching for my Superman when another blind date came along. This time it was Lawrence. I took one look at him and said to myself, "He's Clark Kent, and that's close enough." The guy who fixed us up was a friend of Lawrence's from Harvard. I loved the pedigree—Harvard undergrad, Harvard Business, Harvard Law. But when I opened the door and saw this 6'4" guy, I thought, "Probably went to Harvard on a basketball scholarship." I was so wrong on both counts. He was smart enough to go everywhere but not good enough to play basketball anywhere—including a girls' sixth-grade league, even with his height. But he was handsome and funny with a quirky sense of humor and a terrible sense of balance, and there was an electric energy between us.

Years and years later, I was on a street corner near my office with my two older kids, waiting for the light to turn green as we headed to a dentist appointment nearby. Out of the corner of my eye, I vaguely noticed a homeless man I recognized from my single days when I lived a few blocks away. "Hey, 63rd Street Lady; how ya doing?" he asked.

I couldn't believe we remembered each other. I walked closer and gave him some money. And then, though we'd never exchanged more than a hello before, I felt compelled to introduce my kids. This is what polite people do in New York City, I figured. "This is Lucy and this is Jack. The little ones are home with my husband."

Without missing a beat, like he was playing a part in some chick flick I would never see, he replied, "Wow, I never used to see you go out. You were all work and no play as far as I could tell. I'm surprised you have kids."

Aside from the slightly odd stalker element of his remark, it struck me as quite intuitive. He knew that I wasn't where I needed to be long before I did.

How to get out there:

- **What's the image you're projecting and the story you're telling yourself?** Be honest with how you spend your time, who you spend time with, and how you describe your life—to yourself and others.
- **Could you have met your match already on a mediocre date, and they just need a second chance?** Think about it. Have you ever behaved on a date in a way that you regret or that you know didn't reflect who you really are? So couldn't Mr. Can't Categorically Rule Him Out be Mr. Right?
- **Learn from the guys you know.** I bet they have more fun. The men I know have their "things"—their toys in the garage, the sports teams they root for, the guys they hang out with on Sunday afternoons. They don't convey the sense that they are there by default and wishing they were instead with Mrs. Right. Their bonding rituals may seem less intimate and deep (don't be fooled), but the rituals serve an important purpose. They let men be where they are.

The Here and Now of Marriage and Family Making

A very few number of times, you get to experience a moment that is just so...well, a moment of such contentment and well-being that it borders on the divine. Right then, you need to have the grace to just be where you are—because that's exactly where you are meant to be.

For me, the most memorable of those moments came on my wedding day. I will remember it for as long as I am capable of remembering anything. We got married in November 1993 at the Metropolitan Club in New York. It's a throwback to another era, one of grand opulence. Think the *Titanic* on firm ground. Why I wanted that fancy setting, I don't know. It seemed like that's what you were supposed to do. I wore a whoop-de-do dress I'd never be caught dead in today, but we all make mistakes.

It was time for me to walk down the aisle. I had wanted to walk alone and have my father meet me halfway. The music was playing, and I remember the wedding planner saying, "Wait, wait. Breathe. Now go." In that moment just before going to marry Lawrence, I knew that everything would be fine, that I had found him and we would have a family. It was all going to be all right.

At other times, you end up not being where you want to be, but rather someplace where you never imagined yourself and where you feel you don't belong. At those times, you have to take the longer view and know that you won't always be in that spot that messes your neatly laid plans of how things would unfold. For me, that moment arrived when I had to face the reality of infertility. For another woman, it might be the moment she deals with a death in her family, her own health issues, a crumbling career in a field undergoing massive change, or a child with special needs. It seems that *everyone* I know eventually ends up dealing with things that "only happen to other people."

A couple of years after we got married, I informed Lawrence that it was time to have children. It was something we both agreed we wanted before, so an ultimatum wasn't necessary, but the formal moment signaled a significant change in our relationship. We began the awkward mating that, ironically, we are biologically programmed to do. Sex for the sole purpose of procreation was counter to the way I had been living my life for quite some time. It is also the worst sex I've ever had, though any awareness of that remorse soon faded as we realized nothing was happening.

For the first few months I was relieved. We were still newly married, and just how eager was I to have my life turned upside down anyway? But then the seasons changed, and changed again, and still nothing. I bought ovulation kits, pregnancy tests, and boxers for Lawrence; I avoided hot tubs and biking and drank the teas people recommended. I took any step that could be helpful and heeded any old wives' tales I heard, figuring there was no downside to doing so.

I was crushed when friend after friend became pregnant. While I never thought their getting pregnant had anything to do with my not conceiving, deep down I wondered, "Am I going to be the one, that one, who could never get pregnant?"

My gynecologist suggested we try Clomid for a while (the starter drug for infertility), but if that didn't work, she recommended we see a specialist. The moment to raise the ante arrived after months of Clomid failed to result in pregnancy. There is a divide, a border crossing here. Clomid is like taking a vitamin. It is the last exit in natural conception before crossing over to needles, Petri dishes, test tubes, and acronyms like IVF. If and when it fails to work out, you progress to a new level of stress, desperation, and invasive procedures. Getting to a top fertility specialist in New York City feels like trying to get an audience with the pope. One doctor would open up a few spots early on some Tuesday at the beginning of the following year, for example. And that was just to get the starting consultation. For two type A people like Lawrence and me, that wasn't going to work. We did the "who do we know" thing to figure out how we could pull some strings and shortened the process by a few months.

The transformation one makes from youngish, optimistic married workingwoman in New York City to infertility patient is stark indeed. I submitted to every poking and prodding from so many odd angles that it's hard to fathom. Yet by the end of the analysis, they could find no reason for my infertility. It wasn't really Lawrence either. I remember when they handed him back a printout of a sperm analysis with different components checked off and an overall grade of B+, I could see that he was crestfallen. He was trying to think about who he could talk to about getting it changed to an A– or what extra-credit work he could do to improve his grade. With no firm diagnosis in hand (as is many times the case), I began my rotation in the fertility clinic.

Beginning on day 3 of my cycle through to day 13 or so, my new normal was now daily or near-daily visits at 7 a.m. to the fertility clinic. The third-floor testing area was crowded with 30 to 40 different women of all sizes, shapes, and backgrounds who might never otherwise meet, all finding ourselves in a sorority we didn't want to belong to. Perhaps we avoided conversation as a way to avoid "catching" someone else's infertility or to prove we didn't really belong. Or to pretend we weren't really there.

The daily visit for blood tests made me feel like I was a cog in a factory. It didn't take long for me to realize, though, that the nurses probably felt something similar, so caught up were all the women in our tales of woe that we didn't see the staff as people doing a tough job. Each morning I made it my priority to ask how they were, where they were from, or maybe how their night classes were going if it was someone I had gotten to know. I wanted them on my side. Some extra goodwill never hurts, right?

As unnatural as it was for me to have all these tests and sonograms, plus shots at night, Lawrence had his own odd job to attend to. Apparently, or so he told me, it is rather stressful to have to "produce a specimen" on demand *and* get it into the little cup while someone waits for it just outside the door. He's not that coordinated as it is. But the division of labor (and stress) is something less than fair.

Being engulfed in the sea of infertility is all encompassing. Each morning's plans must allow for blood work and ultrasounds, while each afternoon you want to be available for the call with instructions for the night's drug protocol, and then, of course, you need to make sure you get your butt—or more specifically your hip bone—available for the carefully calibrated shot administered by your partner or you at the exact evening hour specified. In my case, a scheduling miscue allowed me to meet a neighbor, a wonderful pediatrician whom I called to see if she could do the shot. I was never able to self-administer, and I knew she was a doctor (we had chatted in the elevator), though I didn't know what kind. There is also the macroplanning, or more precisely, the macrocancelling. You don't want to plan vacations, weekends away, or really make any plans. Life gets put on hold.

For us, after our first full round of Pergonal (to stimulate follicle production) and insemination (to place the sperm in just the right spot to meet the eggs), I got the early-evening call after a follow-up blood test. I was pregnant! I was told to come back again the following morning for another blood test. That next evening, another call came. They were so sorry. It didn't appear that the pregnancy would stick.

I was crushed and imagined they were wrong in their math. The hormone levels would get where they needed to be. I could do it. I knew I could. But of course, I could not. Now I had to wait three months before I could even try again. All the work, the pain, the shots, the sonograms, the insemination—all for naught. We were right back to square one, with a new worry that I could get pregnant but couldn't get it to stick. It was medical Chutes and Ladders—all the way back to square one.

I remember going to a friend's engagement party that night and being so absolutely crushed that I couldn't focus on anything else. I left early so I could wallow. This was my plight now, the narrative of my life: unable to have children. I sleepwalked through work. That driven focus I'd had for so long was relegated to some lower-rung priority.

As difficult a time as that was for me, it was a good time in our marriage. I felt like Lawrence was so supportive and optimistic and there for me...if I could just get past my own pity. As happy as I was to have found Lawrence, I felt I could never be truly happy until we had children. I had no perspective on it. I didn't see that I had a good chance and just had to be patient. Or we could adopt, but that wasn't on my horizon then, either.

I do believe that there is a destiny to *your* children becoming *your* children, biological or not. Whatever path you had to take, whatever circuitous route, however randomly you met your mate, something in the universe conspired to bring just that child or those children to you.

After several months, we tried again. Back to the clinic regimen. More late-afternoon calls from the clinic with results and drug protocols ("We're so sorry, but...").

Month after month we tried. We did the shots at night, and I did the blood tests in the morning, insemination when the hormones were just right, and then more waiting until the day when we would know our fate. I fantasized hearing the words, "You're pregnant." Yet time after time, "I am so sorry" was the only message I heard. Panic was setting in. Yet the doctor didn't seem concerned. He had said, "I will get you pregnant." Did he not realize this wasn't working? This was our fourth round of trying. I wasn't yet ready to make those kinds of deals, like X number of times before we give up. The possibility of nothing working was just beyond what I was willing to face. Lawrence was optimistic, though. Deep down he believed that ultimately it would eventually work. My normally pessimistic mother was quite comforting. She just knew it would work and kept telling me so. She knew.

At the end of yet another round, I was too nervous to be home for it—The Call. On an otherwise lazy day of a summer weekend, I went to play a leisurely game of doubles with Jeffrey and some guys we knew from business at the East Hampton Tennis Club—anything to put my mind somewhere else.

After the match, I went to the parking lot to drive home. There, standing right in front of my car, was Lawrence. My heart sank, but my mind countered—why would he drive out just to deliver bad news? When I walked closer to him, he gave me a thumbs-up with a big smile, and I hugged him and started to cry. We knew this one would take. (We were too elated to realize this one could fail, too.) The next blood test confirmed that not only was I pregnant, I was quite pregnant—with twins.

The next seven months were actually far worse than the previous few years. The extreme nausea was debilitating, physically and mentally. Then I had a hemorrhage, sending us on another exhausting round of visits to medicals experts. And there was the unbearable tension between the two of us. I pride myself on never having physical ailments, possessing stoicism, and having a very high threshold for pain. Yet I was a mess. Lawrence became anxious and even panicked with worry. He prides himself on being in control of complex situations yet couldn't make anything right. I felt he only cared about the well-being of the children and not about me as a person. We, as a couple, were losing our way. But in the end, at 33 weeks (or *al dente*, as I later described them), our children were born. Jack and Lucy had found their way to us. They were perfect. During those 12 days the newborns spent in the neonatal unit, we had a few unexpected hours to ourselves every night. Happily, we found each other again, too.

After Lucy and Jack turned three, we decided to start trying again. Lawrence and I had made a deal to have one more child. He wanted more than that, negotiating for seven, but I countered with negative two, and we settled on three. But he and I both knew that twins a second time was a very real possibility. In fact, deep down I knew that we were destined for twins again, not just that it was a possible outcome. Back to the clinic we went, and after only one round, I was pregnant again, much to my surprise. Also, much to my surprise, I would soon learn that I was pregnant with one child. Hmm—I didn't see that coming.

Once again, it was a stressful time in our marriage. The 1998 crisis was still very fresh both psychically and liquidity-wise. Our extensive apartment renovation was coming to a close, and we were getting ready to move. Then the weekend we moved, when I was 14 weeks pregnant, I miscarried. Lawrence and I cried together over what would have been.

After six months, we started again, back at the clinic—a failed attempt, then another, and then during the third attempt, I told Lawrence I just couldn't do it anymore. I was exhausted; I didn't want to even finish this round. But something about not wanting to be a quitter made me complete the protocol. To finish the story, nine months later, William and Kate were born. And I was officially done.

I am relieved that that pain and mental anguish are over but so grateful for the outcome. (I never know if I should refer to them as fertility treatments or infertility treatments.) Amazingly, most of the time, most couples get there with a pregnancy and healthy birth, a smaller number arrange for adoption (and the stress and time that entails), and the last few adapt and choose to move forward without kids. Life goes on. It does work out. I tell you this also in the hope of reminding myself that we do move forward through hard times. Some wounds do heal completely.

What to do:

- Laugh about how bad the sex is. Be patient but know that Where You Are may not be focused on work.

- Love your partner as best you can—it will be the glue that will make your relationship and eventual family stronger.
- Embrace the moment and believe that everything will be OK. You just might not know what OK means.

The Baby Arrives: Working from Home Is Like a Sexual Fantasy—It (Mostly) Doesn't Work Out in the Real World

I remember the moment so clearly: the epiphany. I was finishing my six-week maternity leave after my second set of twins were born and was trying to ease back into the professional side of my life by working a little from home. I had set up a conference call with the CEO of a company that we had an investment in to hear how the business was progressing.

I gave myself plenty of time to get ready for the call, which primarily meant telling my two older twins, who were four years old at the time, their babysitter, and the baby nurse for the newborns that I was going to do some work. Then I hid till they got involved in some activity and slyly slinked into the home office and locked the door, aware that I was feeling as if I were cheating on my big twins.

The call started on time, but shortly after it began, Jack and Lucy started banging on the door. At first I tried to ignore them, but then they got louder. Finally, I had to excuse myself for a moment to go tell them to quiet down (I'm paraphrasing, but that was the spirit of the message) because I was trying to work. I could tell the CEO was hardly delighted by their adorable antics, and my credibility as a serious investor was being damaged.

Barely two minutes went by before the ruckus started

again, and again I needed to excuse myself to drag my crying children away. They were hurt, I was frustrated and angry, the babysitter was worried and feeling like she'd let me down, and the CEO was irritated. I don't blame him. I'd blown it. What was I going to do? Pretend the kids weren't mine?

But in that moment of facing my kids from the inside of my locked office, I realized what I should have known from the beginning:

You can't be two places at once.

That's it; that's the epiphany—astoundingly simple, as they all are.

Working from home is the worst of everything. It isn't really working, and it isn't really being at home. You can defend it or rail against it as much as you like, but here's the unspoken truth: You are fostering disappointment from all parties while fooling yourself into believing you've arranged for the best of both worlds.

On the days or half days that you are working from home, you'll get the sense that the office is questioning your commitment. Hell, you'll sometimes question your own commitment, so why shouldn't they? Then you'll start to have this inkling that you need to prove yourself and your dedication over and over. Whether you're in the office or not, you will feel like you need to try to work extra hard, or to at least give that impression. This is tiring. Your kids will sense your distraction and try to call their own meeting with you that you must attend. They'll wonder who comes first—the boss and your emails or them.

In my view, you'd be teasing the kids with your *physical* presence but your complete lack of *mental* availability. They can get used to your leaving the home, but they will have a hard time getting used to you ignoring them.

Work, on the other hand, will likely perceive you to be slacking off no matter how diligent you are when you're home. If you're a mom, your office assumes that you're hanging out with your children at least a chunk of the time. That's the whole point, right—to be with them?

Frustration will abound. Think about it. Have you ever tried to call a working-from-home mother who doesn't pick up the phone? It's irritating to say the least. In my business, some things are very, very timely. I resent (we're being honest here, right?) having to email or call for everything that I could have poked my head out of my office to convey.

If I can't reach one of my staff while they are on a business trip, I immediately assume they must be busy doing business, yet I've been on enough business trips myself to know that the amount of time doing business is a much smaller percentage than the amount of time doing all kinds of other things (driving around lost, waiting in a security line at the airport, finding an Applebee's, or being in the hotel business center trying to print something). And yet I don't mind them not being there. If you had stepped out for a moment to use the restroom, I wouldn't resent that. Yet, honestly, if I don't see your face, or you in your chair, it feels to me as if you're not working. I realize this may be irrational, but I'm not the only one who thinks this way.

I understand technology is changing—there was no FaceTime or iPhones or Skype until relatively recently. But I'm not that old. If you're heading to or are already in a male-dominated field, there are going to be lots of guys (and women) my age and older who feel the same as I do. Here's why: The reason someone works from home is because it's better for them and they want to, *not* because they will be able to be that much more efficient, which helps the organization accomplish its goals, or some other business buzzword lip service like that. And very often the reason it works better for them has to do with childcare. In a male-dominated field, the boss isn't going to have a whole lot of interest in accommodating your childcare situation, your sick babysitter, or your three-day-a-week day-care schedule. This may not be fair or right, but if your boss isn't feeling that the company can get the most from you, it's going to be damaging to your career. Not always, just mostly.

"We were hoping that you could work from work today."

Think about this: Have you ever been at the office and your boss is working from home? Can you honestly say that you work quite as hard, are just as diligent, and get just as much done as when your boss is there? Realistically, probably not. It's that feeling we have from elementary school: "Hey, we have a substitute teacher so it's going to be an easy day and we're going to try not to get that much done." Remember that if you are the boss and decide to work sometime from home.

There's one other point worth making. Sometimes, it's just the random, serendipitous interaction that can lead to something bigger: a connection with a boss, a lead that comes in, a call where you can help out. *Being where you are* is a reminder to improve your odds:

Be around for the chance of a chance encounter.

Those moments can't be predicted, scheduled, or anticipated; they can only happen if you are there, in the office, available at just that right moment. There's a truth in face time.

What to do:

- Give up food, clothing, or shelter to get reliable, loving help—the best you can afford. Make friends with your neighbors, the other day-care moms, and the other babysitters in your circle so you have reliable support and backup plans. Offer those other moms help when you can; you always want to have some goodwill in the bank. On those days when I am going to my son's basketball game, I'll always ask, Who else can we take home? or Who wants to have pizza at our house? Are you doing the drop-off at a birthday party? Always take some spare kids with you. Help each other out. And ask for the occasional favor. It's OK every once in a while; people are glad to help. But don't be overdrawn at the favor bank.

- Save your feelings of being overwhelmed and frustrated for your best friend, spouse (but be careful of dumping all your woes on him), and especially a role model who can remind you of what's possible—*not* your work colleagues or your boss. Kids grow up quickly, situations change, and you get better at handling it all. Accept where you are and know that it won't always be like this.

- Recognize that there still exists a serious double standard, and plan for it. A man who takes a few hours off to go to his kid's soccer game is considered a great dad. A woman who does the same has her commitment to her job questioned. The dad may tell everyone, as he's walking toward the elevator donning his kid's soccer jersey number, where he's going. You can just leave. You don't need to lie about where you're going, but you don't need to advertise it either. Save the jersey for the car.

- Figure out the politics and visibility/availability quotient that works for your office and space out doctor appointments, school meetings, and the like, or bunch them all on one dedicated personal day.

- Don't bring your kids into the office very often—not never, but not very often. They don't just distract you—they distract everyone, and it's not their fault.

Of course, there are always exceptions to every rule. Some situations can't be avoided and you absolutely must work from home. It happens. It just shouldn't be the rule or the goal. Working from home isn't free; there is a price.

Be where you are—it's not as deep as it sounds. It's simple. If you're working, be at work. If you're parenting, be at home. Simple.

The Finer Points

The Truth about Maternity Leave

Never underestimate the resentment your colleagues feel about your going on maternity leave. Your plan must be laid out beforehand, and if at all possible, stick to the plan. While having this child may be the biggest, most wonderful event in your life, it's an annoyance in theirs. The world doesn't revolve around your child. If you're having a very difficult time making the transition back to work, suffer in silence, at least when it comes to discussing it with coworkers. Why? Because your career will never get back on track if the perception is that you're noncommittal about where you really want to be. While you *are* at work, at least give yourself the option of choosing between a career-oriented track and being a stay-at-home mom.

When you are a young married woman of childbearing age, be aware that many employers may not hire you for fear of losing you to maternity leave, likely more than once for multiple kids or entirely if you choose to stay at home. What can you do about this bias? Sometimes nothing. But a few things might help. Find a way to tell the story of how both your parents, your aunt, sisters, best friends always worked. Talk about your goals and what you want to achieve.

One woman I know went so far as to leave her job to find one at another company after she was finished having children because she believed she would always be viewed at the first place as a woman who was likely to become pregnant, and that stagnated her growth.

If you believe you're serious about coming back out of desire or necessity, stay in touch with your business world. Also, be in contact with one colleague who can keep you up to speed—preferably a woman. And don't tell breast-feeding stories to men.

Oh, and one other thing. Maintaining your sanity as a new mom is hard enough—nearly impossible some days. In my experience, writing thank-you notes for baby gifts causes postpartum depression. Just get them done.

Compartmentalizing: The Mental Game to Be Where You Are

Most women I know seem to treat their emotions as sacred. Except for a rare few women, we generally think our emotions should be given free rein because of their sanctity without regard to the collateral damage those emotions may cause. Some women may fall to pieces over a fight with a boyfriend or a sister.

Men are generally very good at emotionally compartmentalizing, much to the frustration of women. If a guy is struggling with his boss, it may be taking a toll inside, but he's likely to cordon off the issue sufficiently to continue with sex twice a week or act like a basketball star and not a loser at his next pickup game on the weekend. It's an art, and a valuable one at that. How many times have you let some issue in one part of your life spill over into the next?

For me, work issues can really set me off. I remember taking a special mother-daughter trip with my younger twin daughter, Kate, then six years old. It was a long weekend in the summer, a much-talked-about trip to Los Angeles to visit my best friend Donna from high school and her children. I'd arranged the perfect getaway: a convertible Mustang, kids' activities, and a "grown-up" outing to a dinner party ending in a conversation sitting around the outdoor fire pit at Donna's. Kate was happy to be there—she could stay up late with my girlfriends' kids watching movies and making s'mores. The pièce de résistance was the suite I reserved for us at my absolute favorite place to stay, the Beverly Hills Hotel. I always feel like I've made it in life when I'm there, since I drove past it every day as a kid and daydreamed about the famous guests I knew were lounging poolside.

On a gorgeous sunny morning of the last day of our visit, I thought we had just enough time to pick up a cappuccino for me and a hot chocolate and cinnamon roll for Kate before we met Donna and her kids for a trip to the Santa Monica Pier for rides and games.

It was a rare Monday morning with Kate. As we waited in line at the coffee place, I got a distress call from work about a company whose stock we owned that announced earnings would be disappointing. Big orders wouldn't be fulfilled on time causing the shortfall, and the stock was getting hit. They put out the press release to inform investors of the change in their outlook. This is known as preannouncing to the downside. I had this "Why do I have to do everything myself?" kind of feeling, even though there was nothing I or anyone in my office could do about it. These things happen, but it didn't prevent me from starting to get flustered and trying to think about who I could blame (an unreasonable response).

By the time I left the coffee place, I was in a mild state of fury; then I noticed a telltale piece of paper fluttering under the windshield wiper of our rental car. The line had moved so slowly due to the oh-so-friendly but way-too-laid-back staff, and I was so distracted by the call that I didn't think to put another coin in the meter. A parking ticket. A $75 cappuccino and cinnamon roll later, my frustration and anger were approaching a boil.

Fuming, I put my phone and my wallet on top of the car so I could put Kate in the backseat, buckle her seat belt, and get myself into the car behind the steering wheel with a few choice words I hoped Kate couldn't hear. With much bluster, I proceeded to drive away. Two blocks later, when I realized what I had done, I lowered my window and felt along the roof of the car. Nothing. I screamed and pulled over to park. Both the phone and my wallet were gone.

My mind jumped to all the hassles. How would we get on a plane the next morning when I had no ID? What about all my credit cards? I had no cash. With no phone, how could I reach Donna? I walked around with Kate retracing our route to search for them. Where they could have gone in two blocks, I didn't know. I became increasingly incensed and out of control.

Now Kate, who was trying to manage her fear, asked in her concerned way, "Mommy, what are we going to do?"

"I don't know; we have no money and no phone," I shot back, really not paying attention to her at all as my focus was taken up with the mess we were now in. "Let's go back to the car," was all I was able to muster. She hurried to keep up with me.

When we ran back to the car after our brief, agitated, unsuccessful search, I saw that, lo and behold, I had gotten a second ticket because this time I had not put any money in the meter. What lesson was I supposed to have been learning?

I screamed again, indulging in my histrionics and not realizing how thoroughly disturbing my behavior was to Kate. She started to cry, and in a way that so clearly revealed the depth of her fear, she said, "This is the worst day of my life. What do we do now that we're poor?" She had visions of us getting kicked out of the Beverly Hills Hotel, destitute and unable to get home to New York.

I hadn't realized how scared she was until she said we were poor. She thought that when I said we had no money that I meant we literally had no money—that I kept all the money I had in the world in my wallet, and now it was gone.

It was only after seeing how vulnerable Kate was that I could get a grip on myself and put the situation in perspective. I borrowed a cell phone from someone walking by to call Donna to come meet us. I found a police officer who let us park with no money in the meter while we searched again around the few blocks we had traveled.

With my wits now about me, I had another obvious idea. I borrowed someone else's phone for a minute to call my phone, which was answered by the hostess at the famous Nate 'n Al Deli a block and a half away. When I got there to retrieve the phone, they said a homeless man from outside had brought it in thinking someone from the restaurant had lost it. I found him outside, thanked him, and told him I would normally have given him a reward but I had no money, and by the way, had he seen a black wallet? He said he hadn't seen the wallet. (I wasn't sure I believed that, but, hey—I was the one who drove away with my cell phone and wallet on top of the car; who was I to judge?) This being L.A., I need to point out, he was the most handsome homeless man I'd ever seen. Perhaps he was some down-on-his-luck actor. It was my year to take note of the homeless man.

Donna met us and gave me some money, and we tried to make the best of what remained of the day while I juggled making arrangements for an overnight FedEx of my passport to the hotel and a possible flight change if it didn't get there on time.

When I got back to the hotel that night, I received a call from a nearby shop owner who had found my wallet in an empty garbage can he was taking in from the alley behind his store, right near Nate 'n Al Deli. He had found my hotel room key inside the change compartment and figured I was a guest since I had a New York driver's license. He insisted on dropping it off. Though the cash was gone, all the credit cards were there, and some faith in humanity was returned with the wallet.

It was one of my least proud moments of parenting. Kate remembers the story, but not fondly and not with a sense of drama or humor. I was disgusted with myself for causing the problem, getting so out of control, and scaring Kate.

The irony is that the cause of the drama was completely forgettable. It was not a do-or-die moment in our firm, my career, or our life—I don't even remember the specific stock. What is indelibly imprinted in me is the fallout from not being able to control myself. I apologized profusely to Kate, who wanted it to just be over, but the truth is I truly couldn't apologize enough. I shouldn't have let any of it happen, and certainly not all of it together.

Every parent (including me, despite the aforementioned

story) knows you need to be able to contain your emotions to spare the children stress, anxiety, or fear. Who hasn't made an effort to hide sizzling or boiling-over tensions with a spouse so as not to ruin a good time for the kids? You know that it's the right thing to do as opposed to letting your emotions flow freely. If you shield your children from fallout over your emotional responses to things, shouldn't you shield other parts of your life from it, too, when you can?

When men segregate emotions, they contain the damage. It sounds cold and calculating, but it works in at least two ways: (1) You don't hurt the unrelated areas of your life that have nothing to do with the issue, and (2) it allows you to put the problem in perspective.

As women, we can use our strength in recognizing our emotions and connecting to the emotions of those around us. It makes us warm and intuitive. We can feel what our kids need even if they sometimes can't express it themselves. We can know how to be there for our girlfriends—to listen, not to solve. We don't want to give up our emotions, and we don't need to.

Though I haven't mastered control, I have come a very long way in the five years since the missing wallet. I say to myself, "Let's isolate this and keep it in context." Putting things in perspective has never been the wrong way to deal with whatever has come up.

Many women will counter, "I can't just act like nothing happened." Well, if the queen of England walked in right then, could you somehow control your bubbling emotions more than you just thought you could? The answer, of course, is yes. You would.

We have the power to control our emotions; sometimes we just haven't developed the desire and the right intellectual response to do so.

Think of your emotional expression as a continuum from when you were a child and had a temper tantrum when you got a broken cookie to now when you have mastered many of the frustrations of life and control yourself when you can. You have the obligation and the wherewithal to compartmentalize. You will be happier, and so will the people who love you.

What to do:

- Disarm yourself with hyperbole or ironic honesty. I never count to ten—it just pisses me off. And telling myself to calm down doesn't work either. It's one of those lines that seems to enrage anyone on the receiving end—me included. Hyperbole or understated sarcasm to reframe the problem is my best defense. Upon losing my wallet and phone, now I might say, "Oh, this is the worst thing that could ever possibly happen to me—worse than cancer, worse than bankruptcy," or "Well, this is not particularly convenient."
- Stop giving yourself permission to come unglued. Having tantrums as an adult is unbecoming, self-involved, and not a sign of your power. If necessary, give yourself a time-out or pretend someone important is watching you.
- Stop swearing. It's the baby step of indulging that gives you a free pass to losing it.
- Try to imagine how this problem will feel one hour from now, a week from now, a month from now.

Ups and Downs: The Saddle Points

There's a life stage that I'm partial to, given the geeky math side of who I am. It's what I call the saddle point. I'll explain the metaphor and then the stage.

Imagine an actual horse saddle and the way it curves around the rider and the horse. The saddle point is the single place where the two curves meet. It's that place in the middle where the axis that connects the back and the front of the saddle crosses the axis that slopes over the horse's back and allows the rider's legs to reach the stirrups. The same phenomenon occurs in nature. On a mountain pass, the saddle point is that place marking the highest point between two valleys and the lowest point on the ridge.

In math, this meeting place of these two curves is the inflection point. In life, I see it as that real yet vanishing moment when the high point of one trajectory of your life crosses the starting point of another that begins to take you in new directions.

Each stage of our lives comes with its own trajectory and its own inflection point—that is, the high point and the low point on that curve of life where things shift. A romance is on that rise to a peak of love and intimacy, and then eases off, calms down, falls apart, or simply finds a lull on a long, long path. Like rolling hills, the peaks and valleys flow, and it's often not clear exactly where we are.

This is the point where I am right now—somewhere on that adventure from one peak to the next. I have learned much in business, raising kids, being married, being a friend, daughter, sister, teacher. Yet I know I have much to learn about the next phase in life. Have I peaked in my career? Or is there yet some other achievement and some deal or opportunity beyond what I have imagined around the corner? Have I peaked as a parent? Certainly the moment is near, since while we are mothers for life our efforts to mold our children probably end much sooner than we wish. Have I peaked as a wife and partner? I hope not, but I can tell you with absolute knowledge that there are parts of my body that certainly have peaked.

Yet I have a stirring for what's new—a stirring for some shift in direction or an aspiration around the bend that will take me from the very sweet spot of right now, the saddle point of being on the one hand truly grown up and happy yet on the other feeling bittersweet and a bit lost about what the future will bring. I may not know where my next peak is, but I have a fond memory of the last one.

Not long ago, my former colleague Silda Spitzer spearheaded a night about women and finance at the beloved 92nd Street Y, a rich cultural community center in New York City. Months of planning went into the event. It was going to be a panel of three women: Alexandra Lebenthal, who founded a financial advisory firm with her father and still finds the time to be a mother of three and a fixture in the society pages; Suze Orman—you all know who Suze is—and me. At the last minute, Suze developed acute abdominal pain and was rushed to the hospital with appendicitis. Needless to say, she wasn't going to be able to do it. Thankfully, Jean Chatzky from NBC's *Today* agreed to fill in.

Then, as if the event weren't already cursed, the rain came—not just a drizzle but one of those torrential downpours that would keep anyone in their right mind at home. I was convinced our carefully planned event would turn into a sparsely attended failure. In my dread, I pictured an audience composed of those seeking shelter from the storm and a few intrepid attendees, like my mother and my colleagues who *had* to be there. It would be embarrassing for all of us.

To my great relief and surprise, we had an overflowing crowd. A bad hair night wasn't going to keep anyone home.

My proud mother was prominently seated in the front row with her husband Carl (my parents had been divorced since I was in college, and she had married the wonderful Carl Hutman in 1998). For weeks before the event, if anyone used a sentence with the word *why* in it, she thought that was an appropriate segue to mention that her daughter was presenting at the 92nd Street "Y" on June 10.

Jean Chatzky charmed even the most diehard Suze fans with her funny, warm stories of her financial waywardness till she got her act together and began educating other women on how to do the same. Alex told the story of her pioneering grandmother who worked on Wall Street and remains her inspiration. At work each day, she sits behind a desk that literally was her grandmother's as she advises her clients (many of whom are women) about planning their financial lives. We all felt that we wanted to spend an hour with her at that desk to absorb even a tiny bit of their collective wisdom.

My role as I saw it was to be funny and to impart some of my knowledge from 20-plus years on Wall Street not just investing in companies but understanding how the psychology of investors impacts their financial decisions. I also wanted to impart the message that women should come to work on Wall Street despite the impression that it is still very much a man's world. My logic was simple: No career path is without risks, so you might as well go where the money is.

The panel crackled with energy, the audience was engaged and hung on every word, and our three personalities clicked. It all just worked. The questions from the crowd were thoughtful, some funny, some tricky. Alex, Jean, and I had an easy flow of who would answer what, and we all could have stayed for hours. We gave the crowd what they came for: They saw women in control of their financial lives and realized that they could be, too.

After the event, we mingled with the attendees. I fielded several congratulations, questions, a few job requests, and, as is always the case, a few people who feel the strong need to tell you their life stories while a line of other people wait. I looked over at my mother, who could not have been happier. Several times I had introduced her and she received many exclamations of "Oh, you must be so proud!"

As the staff began turning off the lights, my mother, Carl, and I got our coats and headed out into the still-pouring rain to catch a cab home. None were to be had, and since I was starving—I had been too nervous to eat and the dress I was wearing was rather formfitting (an additional deterrent to food)—I asked my mother if we could stop at Starbucks or anywhere so I could grab something to eat. As is always the case in New York, there was a Starbucks just a few blocks away. We went in, shook off our coats and umbrellas, and got sandwiches, drinks, and a table. We sat and chatted about the evening. My mother bombarded me with questions: "Was she the one from Penn?" or "Was the one who was sitting behind me the one who used to work for you and left after the baby?" or "That was your show's producer, right?" So engaged was she in my life that she knew every character. And her excitement was all the greater since it all happened at the Y, a joy only a true Jewish mother could really understand.

After we were done, we headed one more time back into the rain on a cabless night. Our only recourse was to walk home slowly, at her 70-plus-year-old pace. My mother was the only woman I knew who would lie about her age by saying she was older than she really was. The way she figured it, you can't do anything about your age but you can make people think you look good for it. From the day after she turned 65, she used to say, "I'm 70 years old—what do you want from me?"

I was quite aware of the feeling that somehow in the last several years our roles had reversed. I now took care of her. That was my job. I don't remember exactly when that switch took place, but I knew it had happened some time ago. Before I had children, she was still the parent. But after the kids came along, things changed—slowly at first, but then somehow it became apparent that the role shift was secure and permanent. I realized I worried about her more than she worried about me—her health, her finances, her safety. The balance had changed.

I didn't care that I was ruining my best heels. We shared an umbrella and Carl walked next to us as we headed the eight blocks to their apartment. I dropped them off, made sure that their doorman had claimed custody of them, and then headed off alone. The few blocks to my apartment in the rain afforded me the quiet time to realize that she had given me so much. She had taught me, urged me, pushed me to be independent, to rely on myself. It had happened: I, and all her daughters, became who she hoped we would be.

My mother died quite suddenly from a severe infection about a year later. I didn't get the chance to have all the conversations I would like to have had with her, or even one last conversation. Lately, I find myself at the low point of sadness and missing her so. I am no longer at that saddle point moment of motherhood where I am both a child to my mother and a mother to my children, sometimes called the middle place. I wish she were here to talk to, to give me feedback (good or bad), to be with me for whatever next steps await, but I also know that I will be OK.

I can be where I am. Yes. And savor the moment for a while longer.

CHAPTER 9

Let Yourself Off the Hook

As a working mother, the last thing you need is to be hard on yourself. As a stay-at-home mother, the last thing you need is to be hard on yourself. As a twentysomething with no job prospects or life partner in sight, the last thing you need is to be hard on yourself.

All of us feel overburdened by the sheer number of things we have to do. When you're trying to manage all the different responsibilities and needs of a family *and* yourself, you can't hang onto ideals of perfection that are impossible to achieve. You'll lead yourself to certain disappointment.

Don't waste even a minute magnifying your perceived inadequacies. You can't do it all. Why berate yourself for not achieving the impossible? Would you really expect the ability to be all things to all people from your husband? So why from yourself? You need to learn how to let yourself off the hook. Figure out how to give yourself some breathing room, do what you can do well, and then get used to the "inadequacies" as you perceive them.

You've got to be the one shielding yourself from expectations, yours and others', and giving yourself permission to fall short of the ideals in some areas. I've said it before:

Protect yourself like you would your cubs—as a grown woman, you're no one's cub anymore.

If you're going through one of those times when you're at a breaking point, see what you *can* change and know that things will not stay the same. Research shows that we, as human beings, are grossly inept at predicting the future and how we'll feel about it. To the extent possible, make things easier and lower your standards. You have to get by on being good enough. There is no shame in that. You will get through the present moment.

Multitasking Is No Tasking

I've done a complete 180 on multitasking in recent years. The concept is an outright lie, and it sets you up for failure. In trying to "do it all," you keep retracing your steps as you switch from task to task and thought to thought. You actually waste more and more time while you put more and more pressure on yourself. The more tasks you do simultaneously, the more time you'll waste.

When you multitask, you believe you're being exceptionally productive, but really, you're fooling yourself. Each time you switch tasks, you have to backtrack a little and remind yourself where you are in the process and what's next. Invariably you are spending twice as much time on parts of the task. In addition, because you're simultaneously trying to advance multiple tasks at once, some failures occur, requiring even more time as you try to address them. And finally, as you continue to fold more tasks into the mix, you don't get the liberating and invigorating feeling of removing things from your to-do list.

So what can you do? Get over your desire to be super-woman and do the following:

- **Unclutter your mind.** What's the simplest, least complicated, easiest way you could approach the task or project? Guide yourself as if you were a kindergartner and break it down. See distraction as the enemy. Don't fall prey to the flashing email or the latest call or request. You'll fall into the trap of doing the most manageable tasks and not the biggest, hardest, highest-stakes ones. You don't want your most important work and tasks to lie fallow.

- **Do one small chunk.** Even 20 minutes or one hour on one discreet task will move that project forward. **Always have something to do for wait times.** Always bring something you can do when waiting at a dentist's office, a doctor's office, and so forth. I usually carry with me stock reports to review or thank-you cards to write. You'll feel a tremendous sense of accomplishment if you dash off a few handwritten notes for people you're thinking about.

- **For one other acceptable variation, you can try my mother's unique take on multitasking:** She used to sit in a relaxing bubble bath while her bras and panties floated around instead of washing them in the sink.

The Don't-Do Plan: Give Yourself a Break

Just because you can do more doesn't mean you should. Women overestimate the negative impact of saying no to others—and also underestimate the positive impact of saying yes to themselves. I'm all for taking on big challenges and aiming for big wins, big goals, and big successes. But I don't say yes to *everything*. (I used to and found myself full of resentment.)

I don't cook. I don't know how, don't care to learn, don't feel bad about it. I don't mind cleaning up, but I'm not cooking. I don't care that I can't be the all-around woman who can be out in the work world and then come home and whip up something fabulous in the kitchen. I don't make "Karen's Famous" anything. I don't even know what a lot of the cooking verbs mean: poach and simmer are too subtle for me. I don't care that my kids make fun of me and my youngest, Kate, says, "No offense, Mom...," which always precedes something offensive like, "You're a pathetic cook." I can't do it all. That's why we have Sandra, our housekeeper, who often cooks for all of us. But if we didn't have her, I'd find some other way around it.

We live in New York City, so we order in a lot at my house. On the weekends or on vacations, if we don't go out, Lawrence might cook, and as the kids have gotten older, he's begun teaching them some basic dishes and skills in the kitchen. I'm glad they will grow up knowing how to scramble eggs and roast a chicken, but I'm happy I'm not adding to my to-do list and need-to-be-good-at list.

I can't make costumes by hand, fold an origami village out of construction paper, do papier-mâché, curl my girls' hair with a curling iron (though I did learn how to French braid somewhere along the way—maybe it was the tennis aesthetic I learned in my teen years of competition), make anything out of clay, or do a makeover. I'm fine with that. I can't play a musical instrument, sing, or set up camp. Fine. I don't feel bad about any of it. I'm never going to live up to someone else's ideal of what a mother is.

I have found the things I do well and easily and I relish these. I play football with Jack and Kate, shop with Lucy, take runs with William while he scooters in the park, organize special trips, plan regular gatherings with cousins and relatives, tell stories—over and over again—of the antics of their favorite Uncle Mark (like the time he got Red Hots stuck up his nose), and teach my kids the meaning of family.

What I suggest is this:

Figure out what it is you do a half-assed job at, or hate, and let it go.

My girlfriend Janet won't play sports with her daughter, my friend Juli will never do math homework with her children, and Tracy, after trying valiantly for years to get along with her mother-in-law, finally just told her husband to take the kids and go visit his parents without her. She should have known there was trouble when her mother-in-law broke down at the wedding, crying tears of heartache, not joy, during the ceremony, wonderfully captured on video.

We can learn something from the business world: Outsource what you can't do efficiently. Utilize your competitive advantage where you can.

I've discovered that when I say something aloud, it takes

on significance and it's much more likely to happen. Decide one thing you "don't do" and let everyone around you hear the pronouncement. You know the honey-do list that women give to their husbands for their weekend chores? Well, make a don't-do list for yourself. You will feel so relieved. You can always change this list, but the breathing room that comes from accepting—even declaring—your limits is liberating.

One approach that works really well is to take on one role you can "rinse and repeat" year after year—say, the school contact tree. You set up a system once and you know exactly what to do every September, with a few modifications for changing technology.

Decide on a certain type of gift that you like and feel confident giving. (Is gift-giving one of the stresses of life no one admits to? I think so.) My editor friend always selects books—*Goodnight Moon* and bathtub books for babies, or the latest travel adventure or chef-du-jour cookbook for hostess and holiday gifts—with the exception of perfume, Chanel No. 5, to mark the birthdays of her women friends turning 50.

Did you ever take on a project at your kids' school that left you without time to be with your kids in order to show what a great mother you are?

Well, how stupid is that? If you're a working mom, you are not a failure if you're not the bake-sale mom.

Guilt is not your friend.

Let someone else do it, and you don't need to feel bad about it. Just make sure that you thank the bake-sale or book-fair mom. Call her up and go out of your way to tell her what a great job she did. If she's like most volunteers, she probably did an outstanding job. Not only will you not be resented, she'll feel appreciated.

My friend who is a morning host on a TV show bemoaned to me the dilemma of how she was going to be able to do the show (with the travel), handle her new baby and her stepchildren, and still be the Girl Scout troop leader. I asked how she could possibly be the best one to be the Girl Scout den mother? It's great to attend the events, but I actually think it makes the stay-at-home moms feel bad. (Although I'm sure there are plenty of different opinions on this point to go around.)

For several years, I was assigned to be the soccer team mom, which meant coordinating drinks and snacks for each game and the annual team dinner with players, parents, siblings, and other obliging relatives who attend. To be honest, I tried to get out of the assignment by sponsoring the team with Metropolitan Capital uniforms, but that wasn't enough. For the annual dinner, I "made" my regular assignment—that is, I didn't make anything. I made myself responsible for all the utensils, plates, napkins, cups, ice, and drinks. I would always volunteer for pizza and salads if necessary. I love an idea I heard about at one school where the event organizers actually came up with specific five-ingredient dishes with recipes and shopping lists all prepared. They added and improved on the list, but the approach took away all the competition (seeing who could do the fanciest, more exotic entrée) and stress so more people could easily participate.

If you are ever in charge of such an event, don't put out a sign-up sheet and let everyone choose. Assign each item and let people switch if they want. Otherwise, you end up with all desserts and no vegetables. Trust me—with four kids, I've been to enough of these occasions to know.

Put It in the Schedule

I know "scheduling" sounds so corporate and calculating, but what if I phrased it differently? What if we called it Write Down Your Priorities in Your Calendar instead of Put It in the Schedule? It gives it a little different spin, but the result is the same.

With two career-oriented parents and four children, I feel as though we have a particularly challenging household to choreograph. But I then realize that every household has its challenges—every single one: there are difficult commutes, working in separate cities, children with special needs, parents with special needs, and every other variation and stress. I remember a discussion with the principal of my children's preschool. It was just after the birth of my second set of twins, Kate and William. She had some excellent advice for me, which I remember to this day. She said that I needed to schedule separate one-on-one time with my older twins to help them make the transition. I decided that I would devote two nights a week to taking each one of them separately out to dinner. For several years, this meant going to the diner around the corner from our house at 5:30 for chicken fingers.

Nine years later the tradition continues, but as the little ones have gotten bigger, they are now in the rotation. So I have dinner with each child once every other week. (Week 1, two nights with the big twins; week 2, two nights with the younger ones.) Our mother-child dinners have now become ordering in and eating in the fancy dining room, just the two of us at the more palatable hour of 6:30 or 7. It's a really important way for me to connect with them and for each child to know that they will have time devoted just to them.

Especially with the older twins, now that going to bed is more about quick good-night kisses than long rituals, dinner is our time to talk about everything from how school is going to what they want to be when they grow up to why I work. While I'm frequently absent from the raucous family dinner in the kitchen, it's a relief sometimes to miss an evening with my delightful brood, who have an inability to use utensils properly and no sense of volume control when they speak. I know our arrangement is odd, but it works for us.

For everything I really care about, I put it in the schedule, whether it's my regular dinner dates with the kids, date night with Lawrence every Saturday, weekend games, recitals, school events, a spring shopping spree with the girls, or baseball in the park with the boys (or the girls, in our efforts to be gender neutral and in keeping with our family's mild sports obsession). Lawrence taught me this. If it's not in the calendar it doesn't exist.

You can't hope the plans happen; you have to make them happen.

Whether it's daily activities, special events, or even downtime to plan and think about your life and your goals for your children, if it matters, put it in the schedule.

Put It on a List

Some people give me the evil eye when I mention lists. I probably would have hexed myself, too, until I became a convert. If you really want to be successful and make life easier, not harder, you have to make friends with lists. Any format will do, from handwritten notes to Google Docs, or Lawrence's favorite—abhorrent as it is to me—Excel spreadsheets. There's nothing like having a place to gather wishes and necessities. Rather than cluttering your mind with free-floating details, lists force you to organize, simplify, prioritize, and actually decide.

The Finer Points

A List of Lists—from Lawrence

1. Emergency list—posted near the telephone in the kitchen and printed out so a sitter (or we) can have a copy to carry

2. Schedules—color coded for each family member, posted on our kitchen corkboard

3. Pre-printed grocery lists—including lunch-bag items on preprinted sheets that have all the foods/stuff we like. When we run out of something, you just put a quantity by it to show how many to get.

4. Gift list—family, close friends, and children for birthdays (even as a reminder for a phone call or a card) and important anniversaries we want to acknowledge

5. Packing lists—for warm-weather (beach) vacations, cold-weather (skiing) vacations

---

6. Tech list—for batteries, chargers, cords

7. Household repairs and projects list—estimates to arrange, tasks to tackle

8. Social and fun list—people to make plans with, trips and vacations to research, reservations to make

9. Lightbulb list—which fixture, and inventory. This is where Lawrence has gone over the edge just a bit.

10. Password lists—this obviously needs to be kept in a secure place.

I recently suffered quite a bit of embarrassment when I sent Lawrence flowers for his birthday to our apartment. The card read, "I have a list of things I'd like to do to you for your birthday. Xo, K." Unfortunately, the card was placed onto the flowers without an envelope—there for all to see. Our housekeeper, Sandra, could barely look me in the eye.

Put Friends on the Schedule

One of the most important lessons I ever learned from my mother was the value of lifelong enduring friendships. There is no substitute. With our closest friends we can fully let our hair down, stop proving ourselves, and commiserate, too. You can be totally free to share the best and the worst of what's happened in our lives. Also, a husband, or at least my husband, can't be everything I need him to be. It's not a knock on husbands or significant others, it's a knock on men, straight men—at least as a substitute for girlfriends.

I've had the good fortune in my life of having the same

core group of girlfriends for over 30 years. As different as we are, we met in grade school and high school in the '70s and '80s and we have been together through everything. Death of a parent more than once, weddings, kids, divorce, career successes, career failures, dysfunction, disenchantment, depression, cancer, new loves, new looks, old flames, and lost loves. Most of the time when we're together, we laugh—at ourselves, at the world, at how difficult life is.

You can't underestimate how grounding friends are. Remember that confidant you needed when you were trying to be resilient? Remember the friend to whom you could show your frailties? Fight the urge to claim you're too busy to maintain the friendships. I love this line I learned some years ago:

> *"If you're too busy to help a friend, you're too busy."*

Friendships are built on a foundation of time. That's why college is such a bonding experience. All those shared moments, conversations late into the night, hours of being together for meals, dramas, and dares are irreplaceable.

It's very hard later in life to build new friendships as the kids get bigger and lives get busier. If you're doing the preschool birthday party rounds, that's a few hours a weekend to chat and build relationships. Cherish that time. The cast of friends will change over your lifetime, but all can be so valuable.

Not all friends can or need to be all things. Lots of us have some fair-weather friends—they're fun and you have a great time with them, but you don't reach out to them at your lowest moments. Lots of us also have foul-weather friends who can really get into helping out when we're in a crisis or need a hand, but the minute things are sunnier, they get uncomfortable. These are friends to keep in our circle, but you do need women who can be both and, just as importantly, women for whom you can be both.

There's a twist on the comfort of friends and the permission we thus grant ourselves to "let ourselves off the hook" and be ourselves. It's the role of friends to tell us the truth. This is the special gift of old friends who may know our parents, our family of origin, and the people and places that formed us early on. There's shorthand there, and it gives us the right and the comfort to say what we really think.

The most valuable thing a friend can do is to tell you something you *don't* want to hear but that you do *need* to know. I have sometimes failed my friends by not doing so because I didn't want to hurt their feelings. For really big things, that's a mistake. I don't need or want someone to agree with me all the time. I don't value it at work, either. (Though I wouldn't mind less back talk from my teenage kids.) I so appreciate and listen when they tell me I screwed up.

For those friendships to work, be a good listener. Listen, listen, listen in every area of your life: your work, your relationships, your children—everywhere.

Making and Messing Up Plans

Friends will let you off the hook if they know you care. But children are different. The pressure and guilt are greater, and our children need us—and need to trust us—in the deepest way we'll ever know.

But if it's not clear already, that doesn't mean we have to attend every performance, game, parents-in-action meeting, or the new tradition of follow-your-kid-around-school day (my personal least favorite).

One good and less appreciated truth of having twins is that each teacher at back-to-school night assumes you are in the other kid's classroom. One time, with yet another curriculum-night visit upon us for our third and fourth child, Lawrence and I felt so tapped out at the thought of facing another enthusiastic get-to-know-you exercise that we literally crawled down the hallway on our hands and knees to avoid being seen through the waist-high windows built for the second-grade kids' classroom as we escaped to our car in the parking lot.

You can't expect to be able to go to everything, so begin with that goal off the table. I try to plan ahead what I can attend. At the beginning of the sports season, I go over the dates with my kids, giving them options for which events they would like me to attend and which ones I can make, and I schedule things around them. This accomplishes two things: (1) Since the games go in my schedule in advance, I can usually work them in and don't need to juggle at the last minute, and (2) since my kids are expecting it, they are not disappointed when I am not there every single time.

If I can't make it, I try to find backup, starting with Lawrence. Since we have four kids, we do a lot of dividing and conquering. I remember going to a soccer game one Saturday morning and the coach telling me that he had met Jack's father the week before. I noticed there was something odd about the way he said, "Jack's father." Perhaps he had forgotten Lawrence's name. I said, "So, you met my husband, Lawrence," to which he replied, "Oh, I thought you were divorced since I never see you here together."

What a sudden realization.

I had never seen myself as half a parent set, or that we were tag-teaming like a couple who had mastered the art of shared custody in order to make our parenting and family work.

The thought stopped me for a millisecond. I quickly appreciated this new insight and explained to the coach, "We're very much married. This is what happens when you have four active kids on Saturdays." I realized we were always splitting up so we could be in as many places as possible. We could hardly ever go anywhere together. In fact, New York City cabs won't take six people. But for us, this is what works. Find out what works for you.

For the times when neither of us is available, I lay out the options: Is there a grandparent, aunt, or uncle? Is the event being videotaped so I can watch it later? Can they do the speech at home for me in costume?

Let's say there is no backup, no alternative, no way to make it up. This happens in life. I try to tell them well in advance and plan a specific time for us to do something fun together that they know is ahead. I try to schedule that special event for a date after the event that I am missing so they have it to look forward to. When I break it to them, I try to let them know that I am really sorry, I feel bad, and I know that they do, too.

What I don't do is string them along in the hope that my schedule will change. That seems to me like just dragging out the disappointment over more time than is necessary. With

my kids, I find that meeting expectations is the most important thing. The firmness and clarity seem to relax all of us.
Change what you can, accept what you can't.

What if you've absolutely blown it? You broke a promise.
You missed the thing you said you would attend. Your meeting went too long and you're late. You didn't remind your
little one of the right thing to bring to school. You totally
forgot to do the favor you said you would do.

Here are three strategies, and I have used each one:

1. **Consider telling white or bold lies.** This is a high-
   risk strategy that can be used very selectively with
   a younger child, depending on their age and the situation. You can simply go on as if you saw it, or
   part of it, getting some details from your spouse
   or other parent. Maybe you were parking the car
   when they blocked a goal. Sometimes you've got to
   go for it.

2. **Be honest about being late or missing the occasion
   but put all the emphasis on the event.** Revel in the excitement or disappointment, or memorable details, in
   as much detail as possible. Retell all the particulars to
   them of what you did see. In the retelling it can feel
   like you were there and you can make a memory together.

3. **Offer a profound apology.** Briefly explain what went
   wrong and your part in it and make a plan that provides some sense of reparation. Arrange to chaperone
   a field trip, if that's not something you do very often, and that would be special. Take an afternoon off
   from work if you can arrange your schedule. Pick up

your child from school for an outing related to the missed activity. And review your schedule for the next month or two to see if you have other near misses you can avoid or plan for in advance.

The Finer Points

10 Highly Personal Rules for Raising Kids as a Working Mother
(Particularly if you have more than one)

1. Make one-on-one time part of your parenting philosophy. (Note parenthetical comment above.) When possible, take them away alone—even for a night. They will always remember it, and so will you.

2. Create rituals. It doesn't matter what—bath time, walks in the park, birthday traditions, holiday observances. If you listen to your kids ("This is what we do"), you'll discover you have more rituals than you thought.

3. Apologize to your children if you don't come through—it's shockingly disarming. (Works well with husbands, too.)

4. Make sure your kids know they are not the center of the universe, and neither are you.

5. Expect to make a trip to the emergency room at least once per child.

6. Chaperone one field trip or sleepover a year. You will learn so much from overhearing their conversations and getting the inside scoop from the other parents. And your kids will love having you there and showing you off.

---

7. Let them see you laugh at yourself often. Let them see you cry rarely—not never, just not often.

8. Let them know your relationship with your partner/spouse is very important to you.

9. Do not answer your phone between 7 and 9 (or whichever window of time works).

10. Let yourself off the hook. You'll become a better role model for your kids and a happier person with more love to give.

Learn from Others and Embrace the Wisdom of Our Mothers When We Can

As a closing note to the way-too-big subject of children, look for simple wisdom that worked for you. I didn't realize it till I was a mom and then a boss—and thus a de facto teacher myself—that the wacky things that came out of my mom's mouth were really "Jane's Life Lessons" that she was teaching us our whole lives. They were just encrypted and I've only discovered how to decode them as I've looked for deeper wisdom and guidance for my children—especially my daughters.

These five lessons may get you started with wisdom you have but have not yet recognized or put into practice for yourself and your family. I've included what Mom said or did and my interpretation of what the lesson was:

Lesson 1: Every night growing up, we'd sit down to dinner, and Mom would announce, "Manner School is now in session." What she meant: It's not just about using the right fork; it's about being polite and gracious to everyone and taking the high road—or being "like Jackie," as she would say.

Lesson 2: Vacuum your kids' rooms while they're sleeping. It teaches them to sleep through anything. What she meant, aside from fostering kids who aren't too prickly about their surroundings, was this: Learn to focus and don't get distracted from the goal by the noise.

Lesson 3: "Play hurt"—as in get right back in the game; it won't kill you. What she meant: You can power through. Don't give up in the face of adversity and obstacles.

Lesson 4: "Enough happiness," she would say. Now, this is a tricky one, and I didn't realize it until I had kids that you need to substitute the phrase *material things* for *happiness*. So the lesson is this: enough material things. What she meant: Give your kids enough but not so much that they don't appreciate it.

Lesson 5: This was for the girls in the family. "When you're getting your hair colored, tell them to do it really blond; it doesn't cost more." What she meant: Get it really blond; it doesn't cost more and lightens up your whole face.

CHAPTER 10

Take Control of Your Money (the New Black)

You would never let someone else, perhaps a man, decide unilaterally where you live, what you wear, where you send your kids to school, or how to vote. So why would you relinquish control of your finances when it affects every aspect of your life?

To think about it another way, if you were diagnosed with breast cancer (and thankfully, 90 percent of us are unlikely to face that moment), would you then say to the doctor giving you the diagnosis, "I'm not going to ask you one question about it or do any work to educate myself about the diagnosis or what my options might be. Go on doctor. You decide and choose what to do and don't go through any of the options with me because I can't understand them?" Or "Doctor, please just speak to my husband (or significant other) about this. You two decide, and I'll willingly, silently go along with whatever you think is best."

On its face, the scenarios I just laid out seem preposterous, and thankfully only a small minority of us will ever face that diagnosis and the conversations that go with it. However, an astonishing 90 percent of women are going to be in charge of their family's finances at some point, whether it's through death, divorce, or disease. Bad things happen. Yet the woman who sticks her head in the sand about finances in spite of her likely future responsibility is the norm, not the exception.

The Freedom of Having Your Own Money—Whatever the Size of the Pot

Have your own money. It's a mantra I heard from my mother from childhood on. In her view, for a woman, having your own money was the secret to life. It was the be-all and end-all that allowed for freedom, fun, and even happiness.

Having money was an extension of her fundamental belief in working as hard as you can in all you do. Whether her eye was turned on her own kids, or all our friends who "benefitted" from her universally applied lessons, or the children she taught ("You're going to learn to read whether you want to or not"), she imparted the belief that all of us could always do better.

For the girls especially, maybe because it was understood with the boys, her lesson was this:

Choose to be successful with money being an important part of the definition, and happiness will follow.

Have your own money. It sounds so simple yet so impossible for some and so liberating for others. Several generations ago, the idea was pioneering. For too many women, it still seems to be. Even when we see the wisdom of having our own money, we may not believe we fit the mold. Money and wealth and freedom are for those "other" women—which perpetuates a myth that for women, having money is optional or unimportant.

For me and my sisters, money was always a primary goal. It came before the other big-picture life attainments that women think of: marriage, family, community. I had to achieve that goal before anything else could happen, or so it seemed. I had to learn to be on my own.

We saw our mother's limitations that stemmed from her feeling that she had less power in her marriage. She felt as if she needed approval from my father for any purchase, and they both believed he should have the final say on major decisions. Wrapped up in this equation was the notion that he was more important—that his opinions, wants, and decisions came first.

Have your own money. This isn't an idea to take lightly or to assume applies to some women but not you.

Why have your own money? So you can buy what you want is one glaringly obvious reason. Whether you have a lot or a little (right now), it's yours to allocate, spend, and save as you wish. Thank goodness most women are no longer at the mercy of "pin money," the term for a small allowance given by a man to his wife for her own small personal purchases. The term actually originated when the wife of Henry VIII introduced pins into England from France and a separate sum for this luxury was granted to the ladies by their husbands.

Another powerful reason is that it gives you integrity and confidence. If you don't have an emergency fund, it's likely you will not have the freedom to do what's right or what your heart tells you to do. My friend Joanna Coles calls it the FU (Fuck You) Fund. I love that. As she explains it, with a small fund, if things get really bad at work, you know you can always walk. In her 20s, she cobbled enough together from freelance work on weekends to know that if anything went really wrong, she could still survive, and it gave her confidence.

Another reason to have your own money is so you don't have to explain or gain approval. While I believe in honesty, and especially integrity, I believe there are limits. Having my own money allows me to lie to my husband at will (till now, anyway, or perhaps he'll let the ruse continue). This has saved our marriage more times than I can tell you. He once found a Manolo Blahnik receipt and was apoplectic. I then convincingly told him it wasn't just for one pair. (It was.) What was he going to say? I was paying the bill. I hide the receipts now and I make up prices for whatever I think *he* thinks things should cost. It's fun.

And there's an even deeper reason: so you have the freedom to not be dependent and needy—psychologically and practically. For me, this is the more complex truth. I have a hard time spending someone else's money. And I know I'm not alone.

In my role as a financial investor and money expert, I often take on the confessor role. My office, or sometimes a quiet table over lunch or drinks, often becomes a confessional booth where female friends, clients, assistants, and industry colleagues tell me their deepest secrets about money. I meet some of the wealthiest women in New York, and I can tell you, they don't feel comfortable spending money that's not their own.

In my world, and I believe in the world at large, money confers power. Maybe it should, maybe it shouldn't, but it does. Spending someone else's money doesn't feel right. I don't want to surrender that power to anyone, so I have to make the money myself. For me, the ability to take care of myself was my emergence as an adult in the world.

My little sister Leslie is the only one of the five of us siblings who is not working outside the home. She was a successful analyst with one of the most prestigious firms on Wall Street before the markets collapsed in 2008. The combination of her becoming a mother of one, then two, then three children in quick succession and the changed environment in the financial markets made the decision to stay home with her kids an easy one. She doesn't regret her choice for a moment but does say she hates feeling vulnerable to her husband. For her, though, having her own money that she was able to save was instrumental in giving her the option and her feeling comfortable enough to quit. For many women, her choice is the road often taken, but in our family, it is the road less traveled.

Have your own money. More than just for fun or a sense of self, having your own money gives you power and choices.

The Money Fairy Tale

Something profound is holding women back from the power and choices that come with having money. Beyond all our excuses and explanations, which we justify as the truth (we'll get to those shortly), there is one huge myth—a fairy tale, really—that is never spoken aloud or maybe not even recognized as a conscious thought that leads women to surrender themselves in the money realm:

A woman who takes care of and controls her finances is planning for failure in her personal life.
A man who does the same is planning for success in his.

I know it sounds awful, but the woman who saves and buys her own home or apartment may be viewed (erroneously) as likely to be forever single, while the man who does the same is just planning for the wife or significant other and family surely to come.

As one fiftysomething woman recently told a financial-advisor friend of mine with a mixture of shame and fear, she earned a six-figure income but was avoiding saving aggressively for her future because it felt to her like raising a white flag and saying to the love gods that she surrendered and she'd always be alone.

We modern women are stuck with beliefs that don't make sense and that don't work. We expect the man to help with the child rearing and to help around the home, so shouldn't it follow that we should expect to help earn the money and manage it for our futures? Should we view earning a good portion of the household income as a sign we didn't marry well any more than he should feel caring for the children means he married someone who couldn't cut it as a mother?

I have never understood why more women, all women, don't want to make money—both earn and invest it. I don't just mean in the way that we all want to be 5'9" and a size 4 (or for the Kelly Ripa fans, 5'3" and a size 0).

Ironically, some women act as if the more money they have, the *less* interested they are in learning about it. In some cases, if a woman hasn't made the money herself, she may feel she has no obligation to educate herself about finances. Does she feel she's made a "bargain" to be taken care of? Or, like my mother, does she feel she doesn't have a right to take a proactive role and be an equal partner? Relying on the man or men in your life is not the solution. They can squander your money, lose it, or leave you alone to deal with it. And you are equally capable.

Men aren't born with a genetic predisposition toward learning about money. The difference is that they don't believe they have the luxury to avoid it. They either learn about it or pretend to know about it.

You must stop surrendering control of your finances to someone else—or to the universe. The universe doesn't have a plan for your money.

The Top 10 Money Traps (and How to Get Out of Them)

All across the financial spectrum, I'm less worried about the glass ceiling and women being too hard on themselves than I am about a glass barricade made of self-imposed excuses cleverly cloaked as legitimate reasons for women not taking control of their money. Sometimes taking control simply means educating yourself and being an active part of the process. It doesn't always have to mean making the money.

Trap #1. It's Unromantic, Impolite, and Inappropriate to Talk about Money

If you and Prince Charming are riding off into the sunset, you may not need to discuss money. In the Magic Kingdom, your palace is unlikely to have a mortgage. For all others, you're living in a fairy tale if you don't discuss it.

You may buy into the myth that it's unromantic, impolite, and inappropriate to talk about money. Perhaps it feels awkward or embarrassing. Money talk will burst the love bubble and raise all kinds of questions of trust and values, and practical things like who's good at dealing with it and who's not. You may believe in your heart that you'll work out any disagreements by relying on the strength of your love and your commitment to each other.

Growing up, you may have learned that talking about money isn't done. You may not have had experience thinking about decisions relating to money, and as a teenager and young adult, you probably weren't even aware of those discussions ever taking place because they were something always done in hushed tones behind closed doors.

This is a relic from a bygone era. Even if you believe that talking about money is unromantic or impolite—which you may—you have to do it anyway. Even if money is harder to talk about than sex, you still have to do it (talk about money, I mean).

Women remain silent at their peril. Too many of us hate to speak up at work, and we may not want to do it with our spouse or significant others, either. Well, we have to do a lot of things we don't want to. Does anyone really *like* flossing? It doesn't release us of the duty.

Money is such a huge part of your life. It's a conversation

(or many, many conversations) you need to have with a potential or actual life partner. It's integral to every major decision you are going to make. You have to know what motivates your spending or at least be able to relate to your partner's motivations and beliefs and be willing and able to compromise on things or it will become an invisible and sometimes challenging barrier in the relationship.

Think of it as the sex talk. Do you borrow money to buy things before you can afford them or stay chaste till the balance sheet allows a purchase? What turns you on? Spending on clothes, vacations, entertainment, home goods? Does being in debt scare you or excite you? Should one of you stay home if you have kids? Does earning money mean you're in control?

Money—earning, spending, saving—pervades everything, from what sort of home you want to how kids fit into the picture. There are potential obligations down the road, like helping aging parents or siblings who hit challenging times, and questions of if and when the breadwinner(s) plan to retire, and on and on.

I will tell my daughters that being poor is romantic for only so long. It sounds awfully blunt, I know. But it's true. While people value money differently and one can be happy and successful across a wide spectrum of income, a good friend of mine captured this reality in a conversation he had with his father:

Father: The best things in life are free.
Son: What about the freedom from worry? Isn't that a good thing to have?

A great first step out of the money trap: Know what you have. Before you and a partner can become a we, you need to know what each of you is bringing to the table. Let's start at the beginning. Do you know how much money you actually have? You'd be surprised how many people don't. Or they know about one or maybe two accounts, but not all the rest. Equally as important, you need to know how much debt you have—that is, mortgage, credit card debt, student loan, home-equity loan, bank loan, personal loan, or debt such as taxes due or taxes that would be due upon a sale. This information is available and necessary. It's so easy to discover if something is amiss and so satisfying to know when things are in order. It's the starting point for everything else. You need to know all this even if you are not in control of the finances.

Next, there is a second straightforward question: Where is everything, literally? Where are your account numbers, mortgage, any other debt or obligations, life and other insurance documents? Which firms do you have accounts with or owe money to?

Think. Right now. Do you know where your mom's will is and where yours is? Can you put your hands on a list of all your checking, savings, 401(k), and investment accounts—including the myriad of passwords?

Have you ever put something away in a special place so that it doesn't get lost, only to realize later that you forgot where the special place is? The happens all the time with paperwork, safe deposit boxes and keys, and jewelry.

Are your tax returns and backup data all in one place? It's awful enough to get audited (and it's not about whether you're a "good" tax citizen or not; it's about tax profiles and odds), but it's less painful if you don't double the time by having your paperwork in disarray.

If you are a young adult, begin to broach the subject with your parents. If you have older parents, find out all this information while the person with this knowledge is alive and fully competent. If it's your spouse who would know, ask. It shouldn't be something for you to fear. If the person had your medical records, wouldn't you expect to have access to them? So why not your financial health records?

You must find out what you have on your own, what you have with your significant other, and what you may be responsible for. It's the basis for all your other planning and decision making.

Trap #2. "Trust Me—I'll Take Care of You."

In our culture, women are sent the message that we will be taken care of. In reality, we tend to be the ones who take care of others at the cost of neglecting our own financial security. Just watch any of the *Real Housewives* franchise, and you'll get an idea of what I'm talking about.

We believe our spouse or significant other who says (or implies) that they are there to take care of us. We believe our parents who often give us a message that they will always be there as a fallback (never thinking that their situation could reverse dramatically and quickly). Even in tenuous economic times, it's easy to believe messages from our company or boss about how valuable we are and that we'll be taken care of.

However, in spite of good intentions, which are mostly there, the actions don't always follow. You can't ever solely rely on the hope that someone else will—and can—take care of you. For many reasons, some perhaps beyond anyone's control, the promise of financial security as part of a relationship doesn't always pan out.

For many women, accepting the "I'll take care of you" message allows them to slide all too easily into the "taking care of others" side of the equation. It is quite seductive for many women to think they can leave behind the pressures of earning a living outside of the home. Being in charge financially is a burden many of us would rather not bear or share.

It can be hard out there. There's stress and competition, confusing politics, and even more confusing rules to succeed. Ironically, I believe, the stress outside the home (even in the worst of economic environments) is nothing compared to the demands of raising children 24/7 and managing a household with no paycheck. That's not how many women see it, but if you have twins (like I do) or two small children and one has colic, you know instantly what I mean.

As women, we can handle stress and we can be earners—even big earners. And whether or not we work or stay home at least for a part of our adult lives, we can have *more* options and more real security, not less.

There's a money side to this default way of seeing things—not just a career side. It's easier for a woman to see her first and primary job as organizing and managing the spending of what is provided, not earning it or investing it. If the income and saving sources dry up, then ultimately she will be left stranded. As valuable as those skills managing the home and children are, they are not enough.

If you feel it's not your place to ask about the family's finances, that it is somehow overstepping your bounds, you're doing yourself a giant disservice. Again, think of the medical records analogy. You should have access to your financial information. It affects you and your children. You need to know if your husband's family is a carrier of something terrible (the family money will run out) or if it has genes for great health (college will be prepaid)—but either way, save and spend according to your means and goals; don't rely on others and what ifs for your financial security.

You may have a harmonious division of labor, where, regardless of your work situation, you basically run the house and he runs the finances. You each trust that each of you is doing the best they can and the "right" thing for your family. You each may have a benign neglect of what the other is doing in their assigned sphere.

One day, though—and statistically this eventuality is very high—you may end up needing to know about the financial part of your life. You do not want to be surprised. Yet it's quite possible for a man to go through his whole life without ever needing to know how to run the house and take care of the kids.

But it happens all the time. The wife only gets the true picture of the financial health of the household (or lack thereof) after finding a drawer of unpaid bills or documentation of a second or third mortgage. Maybe the husband had the best of intentions. But the moment of being widowed and financially ruined is more than one should bear. Addressing the truth sooner (and together) would likely have been better.

My less-than-proud variation on this excuse is this: My money is for me and our family to share and spend now and in our future, as is Lawrence's. But it's also his job to earn and provide the money to ensure our security should anything happen to us, and he should *also* be responsible for the nest eggs for our kids.

I don't know if it's sexist or biological, but I am aware that I feel the ultimate responsibility for the children's emotional well-being. Even though I make my own money and have my own money, and even though Lawrence is as involved a parent as there is, those stereotypical lines of responsibility still exist. In my psyche, he's the ultimate backstop—the buck doesn't totally stop with me; it stops with him. He's ultimately responsible for our financial well-being. It's the myth I fell for. I'm reformed now. I'm responsible for that security as well.

A first step out of the "trust me" trap is this: Figure out yours, mine, and ours. If you and your significant other contribute financially to your household and lives, there's no skipping over it. You need to be absolutely clear about whose money is whose, who pays for what, what are shared expenses, what are shared "extras" (entertainment, travel, home improvements, giving), and what are individual choices and responsibilities.

Is your money separate? Together? A combination of both? Lawrence and I do something that may be a bit unorthodox, but it works. I have my money, he has his, we each invest our money separately or sometimes in things together, or occasionally I will invest for him and the kids. For example, we bought our apartment together 50/50. But we have only one joint account—a checking account for "running our lives." We each fund it with the same amount, and it covers all the shared expenses of childcare, food, education, activities, entertainment, clothing, some charity, and other daily expenses incurred in running a family with four children. We are free to spend our own money as we wish with no approval necessary from one another. Since we have different priorities in material goods, giving to different causes, supporting relatives or pet projects, there are lots of money choices that could cause tension, debates, and simmering fights. Here's where the harmless lying about how much shoes cost comes in.

If you are in a position to have some of your own money to pay for the things that might not be mutually acceptable, it is tremendously liberating. I fully realize most people are not in a position to do this, but if you are, please do it. Even if it's a small amount. That way, one of you can buy modern art and photography while the other is free to purchase a meteorite or a Paleozoic-era bear skeleton that must stay in his office. I'm not naming names; I'm just giving an example.

Trap #3. Women Are Too Emotional or Too Impulsive to Be Good Investors or Planners in Financial Matters

Women may show their emotions more than men, but it doesn't make us less capable of making rational decisions. *The Atlantic*'s July/August 2010 cover story, "The End of Men," reveals a "mirror image of the traditional gender gap: men and markets on the side of the irrational and emotional, and women on the side of the cool and levelheaded."

Study after study shows women behaving more rationally over market cycles than men, perhaps with a biological basis in lower levels of testosterone, making women less willing to take stupid macho risks. Men trade more often, incurring more fees and chasing gains, which, on average, hurts their returns. Conversely, women hold steady, allowing them to avoid selling at the bottom and buying at the top.

The worst offenders who fall prey to the stereotype that women are too emotional or impulsive to manage the finances are women. Maybe it's an excuse or rationalization, but the bottom line is, this stereotype isn't true, so you can't fall back on it. Even if you yourself feel you are emotional and impulsive, you are still capable of being knowledgeable about finance. Even if you get furious every time you come home to a sink full of someone else's dirty dishes, cry at weddings, or can't resist a good sale on shoes, it doesn't mean you can't be conversant and knowledgeable about the basics of finance.

A first step out of the "not good investors" trap is this: Make a financial plan. Whether you're at the "basic" level or a bit further along and more advanced, you can't be a grown-up woman, a grown-up period, if you don't have a financial plan—a plan you understand. If you start with the following short list of must-dos, you are on your way:

- **Change your outlook to acknowledge you are building a financial foundation starting now.** You're not waiting anymore. The mind-set shift is imperative.
- **Pay off or pay down credit card debt.** My girlfriend Janet sheepishly admitted to me that she had credit card debt but didn't want to dip into her savings to pay it off. No matter how many times I went through the math of what a great investment *she* was for the credit card companies, she still felt like the money in her savings account was a safety net. I get the idea of a rainy-day fund (i.e., her savings), but that plan is like working on the weather stripping of your house while your window is open and it's pouring.

- **Save 10 percent of your salary** (and lots more if you can).
- **Contribute the maximum amount possible to your company's retirement option so you get their maximum contribution,** thus making money simply by saving money. To go one step further, review and update your investment allocations.
- **If you have your own business, you freelance, or you're at a company that doesn't offer retirement benefits, take 30 minutes right now to open an IRA, Roth IRA, or SEP-IRA**—they are all easily done, and the primary differences are the eligibility based on your income and the total amounts of money you are able to invest per year. You will reap important tax benefits *and* you'll be building your wealth.
- **Pay your student loans on time every month until they're paid off.** Student loans almost always survive personal bankruptcy. You can't get out of them, so pay them off. The same is true for child support and alimony.
- **Get basic health insurance,** if you're not covered by your company or your parents (if you're under 26).
- **Get life insurance and/or disability if you have children or if you are supporting a spouse, relative, or other dependent.** Unfortunately, it's not something we can get to later, when our lives are less busy. Consider long-term health insurance if you can afford it.

Trap #4. All Women Splurge—It Must Be Rooted in a Biological Urge to Gather

Here's the deal. Some amount of spending is fine. (In fact, America counts on it.) But the rationale that spending is good, makes us feel better, or helps us fit in is actually a financial decision, not a self-help decision. And it's a pretty crazy rationale, isn't it? Splurging may feel like a biological imperative—like eating chocolate—but it's not.

That's what every consumer product company aimed at women hopes is the case, and they are making a pretty good bet. Women spend the most money for pleasure, fun, or as psychological salve at exactly the time in their lives that they should be thinking about saving and investing.

In fact, I've learned that there is a tremendous freedom that comes from *not* spending money. The more my net worth has grown, the less interest I've had in material things and the more I want to save and invest. I don't know why that is. Maybe there's just some comfort in the idea that I could have that "it" bag if I wanted it—I just don't "need" it. I don't mind paying a lot for something that I perceive to be of value, but I really don't do it all that often.

A first step out of the "need to splurge" trap is this: Treat yourself within your means—and always save. Splurge on one "it" item, and have it be your badge of confidence for the whole year, or even several. And if you do get a bonus, put 90 percent away and splurge with the other 10 percent.

Learning to live within your means is the single most important concept to know about controlling your finances. It's the basic concept of inflow and outflow. There is no better time to learn to take control of your finances than when you are young. The lessons are simpler when you are starting out, yet you are building a base of experiences and lessons of hard work to achieve goals (maybe purchasing something you've really wanted) and the habits of saving. Being a saver is empowering.

As a nation, we've done an absolutely terrible job of living within our means. We "need" things now and we worry about paying for them later. I don't know if we collectively realize that kicking the can down the road doesn't get rid of the can. Living within your means is incredibly gratifying.

Trap #5. It's Too Scary to Think About

What in your life have you ever done that has turned out scarier than what you feared? Probably nothing. Public speaking, a vacation alone, moving to a new city, deciding to live with someone or to get married, or even having children.

Research shows that doing hard or scary things actually makes us happier and more satisfied, not less. In psychologist Todd Kashdan's book *Curious? Discover the Missing Ingredient to a Fulfilling Life*, he explains, "Whether it's art, music, sports, conversational topics, or foods—whatever it is—if you view something as new and challenging, you are going to be more engaged and feel more joy and pleasure than if you were in a situation that didn't make you anxious."

Translating this finding in specifically financial terms, although most people are petrified to learn about their financial needs for retirement, when they push through their anxiety, they are much happier. The Employee Benefit Research Institute found in its annual Retirement Confidence Survey that 42 percent of people determine their retirement savings needs by guessing. But the people who have done the actual math are far more confident about achieving their goal than those who haven't. Don't let your fear of money and your anxiety over not having enough keep you from the benefits of actually having the information you need to plan for your future.

You need to access and understand your risk tolerance. Are you more comfortable having a safer stream of income, or do you want the chance for more earnings? And this next point is extremely important to understand: A riskier portfolio (such as high-flying stocks or high-yield debt) doesn't *guarantee* higher returns (or it wouldn't be considered risky); it only gives you the *chance* for *potentially* higher returns. You also need to understand that doing nothing, such as having all your savings in cash and treasuries, carries its own risk. In great inflationary periods like the 1970s, cash does not hold its buying power the way other assets do, such as real estate. You don't need to reinvent the wheel; you can have a simple allocation of some cash, some bonds, and some stocks through either mutual funds or ETFs (exchange-traded funds). You can buy them just as you would buy a stock, but they mirror a broad index of stocks.

Trap #6. You Tell Yourself You Don't Have the Math Skills to Be a Smart Investor

Women are just as capable at math as men. There, I said it. In fact, advanced math is not at all necessary in learning about finance. Eighth-grade math will likely suffice. Over and over we see complex mathematical models devised by the world's smartest financial minds blow up. A good investment doesn't need to be overly complex. In fact, our best ones rarely ever are. A good investment needs a lot of room for error—that's what makes it good. A super finely tuned model just shows me there's no room to be wrong. So, simple math is enough to get you there.

Imagine if you started to learn about money and investing at the age that kids today learn about Facebook, smartphones, and computer games. They're digital natives; the language of technology is as natural to them as speaking English (which is a lot harder than math, anyway), and they're not afraid to learn new things.

With my own children, I want them to go out into the world with the expectation that they will take care of themselves and the knowledge that they can do it. I expect it of the boys and the girls. We teach them about saving; we teach them about spending, interest, and about understanding debt. They each get an allowance. They have to allocate a quarter to savings and a quarter to charity (that we plan once a year), and they can spend the rest however they chose. In highly unusual cases, they can borrow from us to purchase something they want, but they need a plan to pay it back. To be honest, I know that teaching them about the value of money is something we'll have to do over and over before they get it.

The concepts are elementary. But whether we are kids or adults, we need to get past our intimidation. You have all the abilities you need. All that's necessary is the willingness to make a plan.

A first step out of the "bad at math/numbers" trap is this: Get professional help (and I don't mean a shrink). It's not a question of how brainy or adept at numbers we are. We all need help with our financial plans and our life plans. There is no shame or failure in needing help. Not getting help because you are embarrassed about your lack of knowledge isn't a good excuse. I don't avoid taking my car to the mechanic because I don't know exactly how the engine works.

There are many options for paid advisors, but I always recommend starting with the free options. A bit of self-education goes a long way. You went to school to prepare yourself for work and a productive life. If you were one of those no-college-for-me types, you studied in the real world and probably taught yourself a fair amount.

Now apply that to your money and your investments. You can learn the basics by taking advantage of company-sponsored workshops, exploring options on one of the excellent financial websites such as LearnVest, DailyWorth, Fidelity, or Ameriprise with a personal financial planner or investment advisor, or by attending a course at a local college. Even our TV indulgences can be a source of advice. Suze Orman has lots to teach us about money. Taking in a dose of her financial medicine is healthy and entertaining, especially as she dispenses her advice with her trademark humor and realism.

By the way, Suze is the same way in person. I've gotten to know her through our shared CNBC connections, and I've discovered she's great fun in person and always willing to help—whether with a business question or as a friend. I have a special soft spot for her. A few years ago when my mom was sick, Suze heard about it and asked what she could do to help. I took the liberty of mentioning that my mom would love hearing from her. Almost before we'd hung up the phone, she'd gotten my mom on the other line and made her day. It is a high honor indeed for a Jewish mother interested in money to receive a get-well phone call from Suze Orman.

It can be particularly helpful and often necessary to get expert guidance at different stages of life and income when your specific needs evolve. Whether it's buying your first home, planning for your children's educations, or conserving for a relative's long-term care, you can think of your evolving financial plan as a renovation you want to do to your current home or apartment so that it will serve your needs not just now but later on in your life. Very few of us could do a renovation without help.

If you go the route of a paid financial advisor, there are a few things to consider. There are many places to go—some as close as the nearest branch of Bank of America, JP Morgan, or AXA. When you have a financial advisor from those places, they are more likely to lead you to in-house products, such as their own mutual stock or bond funds. These may or may not be the best product for you. Be sure to inquire about fees versus other products not of the in-house variety. Or you could choose an independent financial advisor who charges based on your assets. They will be more agnostic in choosing products. Again, compare fees.

We all need help and advisors, especially when we have new financial circumstances and goals. I've needed help with tax planning, major gift giving, setting up 529's for my children, and estate planning.

Trap #7. You Are Too Old or Too Overwhelmed to Learn about Finance

If you haven't been in charge of your money or an equal partner in decision making, you may feel it's too late. Why start now? If this isn't your situation, it could be your mother's, your sister's, or your best friend's.

For women who become widowed, the period around their spouse's death is so jarring that it seems to be an almost biblical burden that their moment of grief is when they must take responsibility for the family's finances. I liken it to the commonplace occurrence of having a baby by caesarean. The day a new baby arrives into a home and family is a really inconvenient time to have major abdominal surgery, yet it happens all the time. Nobody asks us when it would be convenient to learn about finances, but life's unexpected moments don't care whether it's convenient or not.

As long as I am mentally capable, I would never want to burden my children with my financial well-being. I don't think it's fair for me or for you. I believe you need to take some responsibility for your own finances. You are never too old to learn. The basic principles are the same today as they were 100 years ago, though perhaps they have different names.

A first step out of the "overwhelmed" trap is this: Develop a financial identity when you're young if you can. If you are single, your accounts are all in your own name, including your lease, mortgage, credit cards, and even phone bills. For women who run the household and don't have independent earnings, and even for women who do, you may not realize that your credit card isn't under your own name and that you have no built-up credit of your own. You may discover that you can't access information about your account because the account is listed under your spouse's name and from the company's perspective you are an unauthorized user.

Things happen: health emergencies, relationship crises, financial reversals. Make sure you are a cosigner, co-owner, or independent cardholder or account holder so you have a financial identity of your own, can protect your funds and credit rating, and have access to your money whenever it is necessary. You need to build on your own financial identity, even if you think you won't possibly ever need it.

Trap #8. Marry a Wealthy Guy and You Are Set for Life

Wealthy self-made guys are often powerful guys who are accustomed to getting what they want. It might seem quite intoxicating to be with them when you're the one they want, but from what I've seen, and I don't know why, the richer and more powerful they get, the less committed they can be, leaving too many women vulnerable.

Then there are the men who are born wealthy. This comes with a whole different set of issues. Often the money comes with strings, real or imagined. There can be a barrier to discussing the family wealth with the matriarch or patriarch and you may be seen as a gold digger if you wish to do so. So while it sounds nice, be aware that it's not all it's cracked up to be.

If you were to divorce or if he were to die, it's quite possible that you wouldn't have access to any of that money—even if your children do. Having your own money neutralizes so many things. A first step out of the "marrying for wealth" trap is this: Start with traps #1 and #2. Find out what you have and where it is. You'll feel calmer and immediately more empowered.

Trap #9. You're Comfortable Enough Financially, so It's OK to Be Complacent

Maybe you have some family money. Maybe you've made some money, have started to save and are building a meaningful nest egg, and assume that it will continue that way and you can get to planning for future retirement later. Maybe you think your life is going in all directions and any plans seem like a shot in the dark, so why bother and worry about that now? There is always going to be some reason that sounds legitimate and logical for why you should put off thinking about your money.

For many years, I felt overwhelmed by my work, my young kids, and my to-do list. I was the quintessential career woman crazed with trying to keep all the balls in the air.

On the financial front, it was a big accomplishment when I'd transfer money from my checking to my savings account—never mind the fact that I had no long-term investing plan beyond investing in my fund. I constantly felt guilty about not having an up-to-date will, but every spare moment seemed to be spent working and arranging and managing. I felt I had my hands full. One day I had a wake-up call talking to my partner about some planning he was doing for his family and some investments he was making. If he found the time to do it, I should as well. His approach seemed so smart—and so important and so proactive. No one was forcing him to do it. Intellectually, I'd always known I should be looking ahead, but suddenly it hit me: Who's in charge of my financial well-being and planning? I am. I had to start now. Yes, I was comfortable financially, but I could no longer be complacent.

That day, I started to put our personal financial plan in order by moving it from the to-do to the must-do list.

The other items on the to-do list—things for the apartment, gifts to buy, social plans to make—could suddenly wait another day, week, or month.

Our daily busy-ness and the constant minor tasks we need to attend to can make big-picture planning seem impossible. It doesn't matter how immersed you are in the business side of business or how much money you have, just like the doctor who never gets a checkup, too many of us fail to make the time to address our money issues. Yet it must be done. If you are waiting for a vast empty space in your calendar that says "learn about finance here"—with an entire 30 days clear for the project—it isn't going to happen.

A first step out of the "complacent" trap is this: Take a seat at the money table.

Once you've finally gotten to the point where you have a nice life, the thought of losing it is more unbearable than if you'd never gotten there. That's why this is the moment where you need to safeguard what you and your spouse have built.

Ignorance is not bliss. It is ignorance. It is also not fair to have the burden of every major financial decision resting on one party's shoulders. Everyone needs a sounding board and even a skeptic—especially if you don't know what you're doing, and very few of us always know what we're doing.

I meet with a lot of women who find themselves much less well off than they thought they were when their husband's get-rich-quick scheme or sure thing turned out to be not such a sure thing after all. The one that stands out most in my mind is the woman who was divorcing her husband for, among other things, the financial ruin he brought upon them when the Chinese pig farm that he invested most of their money in went "belly-up." He had no experience in Chinese investments and no experience in pig farms, yet together those two elements couldn't lose.

Sometimes one of you just needs to ask the question, "What position will we be in if this doesn't work out?" The way I think about such things when I make investments for the fund is, "I have to look down before I can look up."

Trap #10. You Don't Have Enough to Make Any of This Relevant

To state the obvious, you start with what you have and you make a habit for a lifetime.

If you have $200 and want to start to invest, that's enough to open a commission-free starter account.

The same thing goes for young girls who are babysitting or have their bat mitzvah or quinceañera or sweet sixteen money. You can take a quarter or half and open your first investment account.

If you're in the work world and getting by, perhaps climbing the professional ladder or trying to, you might not see yourself as someone who has anything to invest. Yet you do. The small amounts you set aside early can turn into substantial amounts over the years. These savings also provide a buffer if harder times come. Waiting for your big break and the bigger salary isn't the right plan. Give yourself the pride and security you deserve. Thinking about money and wealth and building on what you have is not something you need to eventually get to; it's something you need to start.

A first step out of the "not ready" trap is to start small now and learn by doing. Here is perhaps the single most important concept to taking control of your finances: There are two parts to a financial picture—money in and money out. Very often the money-out portion is the one where you have much more control.

There isn't a single one among us who couldn't find a way to spend less and invest more. It allows you to take the first steps toward implementing a financial plan and funding a portfolio. Once you begin building your nest egg, you will want to continue to see it grow.

There is a discipline to putting away something from each paycheck into savings right away and spending the rest that is so helpful—more helpful, by a lot, than spending as you wish and then putting what's left over into savings. (Is there ever any left over?) You need to look at it the other way around: How can I make the budget work after I put X amount into savings each month? *Not*, How can I save, if I need to spend Y each month?

Don't Be Your Own Worth Enemy

All these excuses resonate with some of us at least some of the time. They may resonate with men, too, but most men don't allow themselves to surrender to them, and neither should you. You need to get past your money excuses and the fairy tales you hold onto and get a money plan.

As a friend blurted out to me not long ago, "I can't continue to be my own worth enemy."

The Man that Got Away

We have a really crappy car. Why? We don't care about it or what happens to it. We never worry where we are going to park it. If it gets dinged, we don't care. Our kids are embarrassed about it, but we love that. It's liberating. I always thought I'd have a red Ferrari, California girl that I am, yet by the time I could afford one, the feeling had passed. It's a transition from being controlled by money and wants to being in control of money.

I had discovered that genuine luxury was freedom from worry, not 3,000 pounds of Italian steel with a creamy leather interior. My definitions of success and happiness changed, too, as I journeyed from the girl parroting Muhammad Ali in my eighth-grade student council election to the CEO of a hedge fund that on any given day has hundreds of millions of dollars working in the market. The best way I can describe this epiphany is with a story about a guy that I've never even told my husband about.

When I was a junior in college, I spent a semester abroad in London, learning absolutely nothing at the London School of Economics. It was a time for me to travel and explore museums because I wanted to, not because I had to. Before that year, museums were always associated with boredom and exhaustion, not excitement and invigoration. I went to see Monet's *Water Lilies* at the National Gallery, Roy Lichtenstein's *Whaam!* at the Tate, and everything in between. I find something uplifting, joyous, and irreverent in modern art, whereas I harbor the stereotype of older art as stifled religious works or portraiture that's boring even if technically masterful.

In my travels, I saw an extraordinary show called *Hockney Paints the Stage* at the Hayward Gallery. It was not just a mere show of paintings on a sleek gallery wall; it was a massive installation. It was exactly as advertised. There were several huge painted stage sets, more like giant dioramas. There were black-floored forests with ramps and swirls and colorful anthropomorphic trees. There were masks and costumes that had the whimsy of a child's imagination. It was transforming to see how he brought to life this forest in a texturized colorized way that reimagined what an opera stage could look like.

It was that August day in London when I fell in love with modern art. There was a painting in the show called *Mr. Arithmetic.* I bought several postcards of it and said to myself, "One day, I will have *Mr. Arithmetic.*" I loved his irreverent disregard for the rules of math that I was so steeped in. The painting was for the set of a one-act children's opera, *L'enfant et les sortilèges: Fantaisie lyrique en deux parties* (The child and the spells: A lyric fantasy in two parts)—I had no idea what that meant, either—with music by Maurice Ravel and the libretto by Colette. Hockney described the story and the character Mr. Arithmetic like this:

Out of a lesson book jumps a noisy, crooked little schoolmaster character, Mr. Arithmetic, who starts rapidly reciting arithmetical problems, and also out of the book jump a lot of numbers. To the little boys delight, the numbers run around shouting 5 times 4 is 36, 6 times 2 is 94 and so on. The little boy is so thrilled with this, naturally, he runs around shouting all the wrong sums as well.

Fast-forward more than 20 years to an art gallery in the Upper East Side of New York. Another Hockney show. It included works from the span of his life—a portrait from the famous Celia series with his Picassoesque perspective of her, a flat pool painting from the 1960s, and a colorful landscape from the early 2000s. It was like visiting an old friend. We'd known each other in London, and I had the excitement of rekindling a love affair from long ago that had left me with fond feelings and memories that made me smile.

Honestly, though, I wasn't loving the show in the way I had anticipated, but I didn't want to be rude to the memories, so I slowly walked from wall to wall, trying to take in each piece and notice it for its Hockneyness. The vivid primary colors were there, and the painting contained the wit and whimsy that are Hockney signatures, but my passion was gone. I think I felt the way my literature-major friends sometimes feel when they re-read a book from their college years that they had underlined, dog-eared, and exclamation-pointed and find it has lost its romance and meaning in middle age.

As I dutifully turned around the last corner, ready to leave once I gave a rudimentary glance to the final piece in the show, I saw it—just a flash, and then I looked again. There it was: *Mr. Arithmetic*. I couldn't believe my eyes. I hadn't forgotten about the painting that had made such an impression on me; I just hadn't ever thought that I would come in contact with it again. This time, however, I recognized what I had loved about it, but it was a small painting that didn't have the magic and vibrancy that so excite me about his best work. Looking at it again, at a different time in my life, I no longer felt what I had before.

The art market had been good to David Hockney, and the price listed subtly at the front desk for *Mr. Arithmetic* had many more zeroes than it would have had during my student days (though I wouldn't have looked back then). Still, financially speaking, even at its new, highly inflated price, it would have been a wise investment. But I wasn't feeling the love with *Mr. Arithmetic* anymore, so I passed on it.

It ruins what could have been a good story of a young woman traveling through London and falling for a man (Mr. Arithmetic), only to have a chance encounter with him a quarter century later in New York City that would lead to them ending up together, forever. I thought long and hard about buying it, even telling myself the story in my head, but in the end, I had to let him go. It was part of my past, and the pleasure wasn't going to be there. I let that story, that investment, that wishing go and left room for something that would matter more.

Ah, but it's so nice to know that I could have, if I'd wanted to. There are certain things we buy that give us so much pleasure—from a perfect article of clothing, to our first grown-up resort vacation, to our first condo or our dream home, to the party we throw for our parents, to a first suit for a son. When we have chosen to save for those things and are actively saving for our and our family's future, our money becomes our ally. It gives us the freedom to take care of others and ourselves and the security to enjoy what we have within our means.

Money isn't everything, nor is success, but when used wisely—for what matters most to us—they both create choices and options. Seizing all the moments you can—that lesson to *be where you are*—lets you seize the moments of joy before moving on.

Waiting and hoping for success to happen—in work, love, family, and friends—isn't a plan. Working at success in all life's arenas—reaching for it, strategizing about it, expecting it—gives you so many more chances (options) for happiness. And you know how I love options.

So get out of your own way, push through your doubts and fears, know you will live through failure, learn all you can from it, and thrive. Be bold (bolder than you believed you could be, or fake it till it's real), be confident, and be easier on yourself. And tell me about what happens. I can't wait to hear.

Onward.

Acknowledgments

Some wise woman once said it takes a village to raise a child. It took just a borough of New York City to write a book.

Let me start with profound thanks to Jeffrey, my lifelong friend who is so generous in spirit, in action, in teaching. There isn't space or time to list all the things I'm grateful to you for, but what stands out the most is the lesson you demonstrate so well: being the last to take credit and the first to take blame.

To Janet Goldstein, who was there every second along the way, guiding, interpreting, herding, and listening. I have learned tremendously from you—what a gift that is.

To John Brodie, the sharpest dresser with the sharpest editing pen I've ever known—thank you for believing you could turn a hedge fund manager into a writer.

To everyone at CNBC. First to Susan Krakower and Mary Duffy—you found me and gave me the chance. No one is better than you two at just getting it done. I am so thankful for you both. To John Melloy and Lydia Thew—I don't know how you pull it off every day, but you are masterful. To Melissa Lee—I'm in constant admiration of your hard work, intellect, and ability to think on your feet, all with one eye on the clock. You are the perfect mix of smart and funny and beautiful. To my CNBC boys—Guy Adami, Tim

Seymour, Pete Najarian, Joe Terranova, Jon Najarian, Brian Kelly, Dylan Ratigan, and Jeff Macke: You've taught me so much more than I ever knew I didn't know, all while laughing at ourselves and each other. There's no better way to spend the 5–6 p.m. hour, our happy hour.

To everyone at Metropolitan Capital—Tracy Young, Dora Vardis, Mary Ellen Curran, Greg Drechsler, Carrie Schwarz, Adam Crocker, and Berna Barshay: It is my honor that you share each day with me, and I am grateful. And special thanks to Katharine Heller, who I send on a wild scavenger hunt every day and she always finds a way to get to the end of the list.

To the editing/reading/re-reading team: my sister Stacey, my sister-in-law Lisa, and Mel Berger, my agent. Mel, I can withstand some criticism, really. And thank you for your sage advice at every turn.

To Silda Spitzer, the most gracious woman I've ever known. You got this going.

To my siblings Wendy, Mark, Leslie, and Stacey for being open and honest examples of how to get where you want to go. Since we lost our mom, we've refound each other in a far deeper way.

Thank you, Dad and Sharon, for your quiet confidence and unflappable calm.

To the other Sharon, my mother-in-law, for showing what bravery and perseverance look like.

To Carl Hutman for being so kind to my mother. You two were good together.

To Juli Garey, Janet Eisenberg, and Donna Broder for being everything that girlfriends could ever be, to your dark senses of humor, love of laughter, and storytelling mastery. We have saved each other again and again.

To the family at the center of my life: Lucy, for her strong spirit and sense of self; Jack, for his big, warm, puppylike joy; William, for his dry sense of humor and affection; and Kate, for her *joie de vivre* and intuition. And finally, to Lawrence—for pushing me to go beyond where I think I can, all because you believe it can happen or you make it happen. With deepest love, always.

—K

Index

INDEX

lists and, 204–5
personal qualities of, 87, 171
starting family and, 161, 166, 169–74
Golub, Sharon (KF's mother-in-law), 41, 171
gossip, 62
gray area, 95, 107–10, 115
guilt, 9, 200–202
gut reaction, 53, 103

hair, 104, 105
blond coloring of, 213
styling of, 33
happiness, 3, 4, 9, 15
changed definitions of, 243
money and, 215–16, 246–47
Happiness Project, The (Rubin), 146
Harvard University, 38, 165
Hawthorne Elementary School, 17–18
Hayward Gallery (London), 244
health insurance, 230
hedge funds, 2, 20, 44–46, 59, 126–34
infancy of, 86
mystery of, 118
new high ground and, 150
starting business in, 83, 84, 86
wrong "hedges" and, 130–31
See also Metropolitan Capital Advisors LP
help, asking for, 101
Hockney, David, 244–46
Hockney Paints the Stage (art exhibit), 244
Hollywood, 1, 21–26
home ownership, 154
honesty, 210, 217
hubris, 130, 134
humor, sense of, 139
Hutman, Carl (KF's stepfather), 191, 192, 193
hyperbole, 188

Icahn, Carl, 102
I Feel Bad About My Neck (Ephron), 34
independence, 4, 193
infertility, 20, 90–91, 159, 167–74
treatment for, 9, 91, 168–71, 173–74
inflation, 233
inflection point, 189
information
decision making and, 111, 113, 115
succinct presentation of, 48

insider trading, 7, 56
integrity, 216, 217
interest rates, 92, 129
Internet, 120, 121
financial websites and, 235
online dating and, 162–63
working from home and, 177–78
Internet bubble, 153–59
interns, 21–24, 70–71
investments, 4, 9
asymmetric risk and, 72–91
best risk-reward potential for, 118–19
building nest egg and, 241–42
consideration of improbable and, 82
conveying confidence and, 44–48
cutting losses and, 114, 134
failures and, 128–29, 130–31
gender and, 134, 228–36
hubris and, 130, 134
inadvertent risks and, 135–36
IPO quick turnover and, 154–55
learning about, 234–36
learning from mistakes and, 133, 136, 147–48
long-term vs. short-term, 135
new high ground concept and, 150
professional help with, 234–35, 236
quality over price and, 133
quick changes in markets and, 152
revisiting with fresh eyes of, 150–51
risk and, 45, 82, 92, 233
starting small and, 241–42
trophy properties and, 53–54
underlying value and, 44–45, 71, 153
unfashionable companies and, 157–58
valuation of company and, 51–53
See also hedge funds; stock market; value investors; trading stocks
iPhones, 177
IPO (initial public offering), 154–55, 156, 158
IRA plans, 230
Ironman competition, 3

Jack (KF's son), 8, 11, 48–49, 99, 175, 199
birth of, 173
scheduled one-on-one time with, 202, 203
James, Tony, 56
"Jane's Life Lessons," 212–13 (*see also* Finerman, Jane)

257

KAREN FINERMAN is the CEO of Metropolitan Capital Advisors, a New York based hedge fund that she co-founded in 1992 with Jeffrey Schwarz. In addition to running Metropolitan Capital, she is a regular on CNBC's *Fast Money*. She is on the board of the Michael J. Fox Foundation for Parkinson's Research and is a trustee of the Montefiore Medical Center in the Bronx. She lives in New York City with her husband, Lawrence Golub, and their two sets of twins, Lucy and Jack, and William and Kate.